THE PEARL

John Steinbeck

SPARK PUBLISHING

© 2002, 2007 by Spark Publishing

All rights reserved. No part of this publication may be reproduced, stored in a retrieval system, or transmitted, in any form or by any means, electronic, mechanical, photocopying, recording, or otherwise, without prior written permission from the publisher.

SPARKNOTES is a registered trademark of SparkNotes LLC

Spark Publishing
A Division of Barnes & Noble
120 Fifth Avenue
New York, NY 10011
www.sparknotes.com

ISBN-13: 978-1-4114-0724-4
ISBN-10: 1-4114-0724-5

Please submit changes or report errors to www.sparknotes.com/errors.

Printed in the United States

10 9 8 7 6 5 4 3 2 1

Contents

CONTEXT	1
PLOT OVERVIEW	3
CHARACTER LIST	7
ANALYSIS OF MAJOR CHARACTERS	9
KINO	9
JUANA	9
THE DOCTOR	10
THEMES, MOTIFS & SYMBOLS	11
GREED AS A DESTRUCTIVE FORCE	11
THE ROLES OF FATE AND AGENCY IN SHAPING HUMAN LIFE	11
COLONIAL SOCIETY'S OPPRESSION OF NATIVE CULTURES	12
NATURE IMAGERY	12
KINO'S SONGS	13
THE PEARL	13
THE SCORPION	14
KINO'S CANOE	14
THE STRUGGLE TO PRESERVE VIRTUE	16
THE FALLACY OF THE AMERICAN DREAM	16
THE EFFECTS OF COLONIALISM ON NATIVE CULTURES	17
GREED IS THE ROOT OF ALL EVIL	17
SUMMARY & ANALYSIS	19
CHAPTER 1	19
CHAPTER 2	22
CHAPTER 3	24
CHAPTER 4	28
CHAPTER 5	31
CHAPTER 6	34
IMPORTANT QUOTATIONS EXPLAINED	41
KEY FACTS	47

STUDY QUESTIONS	51
HOW TO WRITE LITERARY ANALYSIS	**53**
THE LITERARY ESSAY: A STEP-BY-STEP GUIDE	53
SUGGESTED ESSAY TOPICS	65
A+ STUDENT ESSAY	66
GLOSSARY OF LITERARY TERMS	68
A NOTE ON PLAGIARISM	70
REVIEW & RESOURCES	**71**
QUIZ	71
SUGGESTIONS FOR FURTHER READING	76

Context

JOHN STEINBECK WAS BORN in Salinas, California, in 1902. He was the third of four children and the only son of John Steinbeck, Sr. and Olive Hamilton Steinbeck. Growing up in a rural valley near the Pacific coast, Steinbeck was an intense reader, and both his father, a local government official, and his mother, a former schoolteacher, encouraged his literary pursuits. In 1919 he graduated from Salinas High School and matriculated at Stanford University, where he studied literature and writing.

In 1925, without a degree, Steinbeck left Stanford to pursue work as a reporter in New York City. He returned to California the following year, supporting his endeavors at writing with a steady income from manual labor. Over the next several years his literary career gained momentum with the publication of his first novels. Although his first three—*Cup of Gold*, *The Pastures of Heaven*, and *To a God Unknown*—were critical and commercial failures, he achieved major success in 1935 with the publication of *Tortilla Flat*, a collection of stories about the ethnic working poor in California. During this time, Steinbeck began to gain recognition from critics for his short stories.

Steinbeck's extensive travels in the 1930s partly inspired two of his finest works, *Of Mice and Men*, in 1937, and *The Grapes of Wrath*, in 1939. Both novels, fictional portraits of the western United States during the Great Depression, are still read widely. Steinbeck received the Pulitzer Prize for *The Grapes of Wrath* in 1940.

Steinbeck's simple, touching novella *The Pearl* originally appeared in the magazine *Woman's Home Companion* in 1945 under the title "The Pearl of the World." The story explores the destructive effect of colonial capitalism on the simple piety of a traditional native culture. Set in a Mexican Indian village on the Baja Peninsula around the turn of the century, the novella tells the story of Kino, an Indian pearl diver who discovers a massive, beautiful, and extremely valuable pearl. The pearl fills Kino with a new desire to abandon his simple, idyllic life in favor of dreams of material and social advancement, dreams that run headlong into the oppressive resistance of the Spanish colonial powers that top the social hierarchy of Kino's world.

While less complex than Steinbeck's other works, *The Pearl* ranks among his most popular, and it is certainly one of his most accessible. The novella was originally conceived as a film project (and was in fact made into a motion picture in 1948); it features a simple, visually evocative style that in many ways recalls the narrative flow of a film. Additionally, *The Pearl*'s simple prose style echoes the traditional style of a moral parable, particularly the biblical parables of Jesus. The story clearly owes a great deal to the biblical story of the pearl of great price, and to a certain extent the familiar rhythms and easily understandable moral lessons of the novella help to explain its continuing power and its long-standing popularity.

The Pearl is not among Steinbeck's most critically acclaimed works, but it has exerted a certain amount of influence in American literature. Its evocation of natural beauty and its use of the short, simple parable form may have influenced Ernest Hemingway in writing *The Old Man and the Sea* (1952). Because of its overwhelming popularity, Steinbeck reissued *The Pearl* as a single volume in 1947, and it has enjoyed a healthy readership ever since. Other widely read Steinbeck titles include *Cannery Row* and *The Red Pony*, both published in 1945, *East of Eden* (1952), and the unique travelogue *Travels with Charley* (1962).

Steinbeck was a prolific and popular writer, but few consider him to be an American writer of the absolute first rank. Whereas most of Steinbeck's contemporaries—Hemingway and William Faulkner, for example—wrote in clear and consistent styles, making it easy to identify their artistry, Steinbeck never stuck with one style, and his choice of narrative form varied greatly from work to work. Nevertheless, Steinbeck received the Nobel Prize for literature in 1962, and although the quality of his writing suffered a precipitous drop in his final years, he left behind a body of work that marks him as a significant twentieth-century American voice.

Plot Overview

KINO, JUANA, AND THEIR INFANT SON, Coyotito, live in a modest brush house by the sea. One morning, calamity strikes when a scorpion stings Coyotito. Hoping to protect their son, Kino and Juana rush him to the doctor in town. When they arrive at the doctor's gate, they are turned away because they are poor natives who cannot pay enough.

Later that same morning, Kino and Juana take their family canoe, an heirloom, out to the estuary to go diving for pearls. Juana makes a poultice for Coyotito's wound, while Kino searches the sea bottom. Juana's prayers for a large pearl are answered when Kino surfaces with the largest pearl either of them has ever seen. Kino lets out a triumphant yell at his good fortune, prompting the surrounding boats to circle in and examine the treasure.

In the afternoon, the whole neighborhood gathers at Kino's brush house to celebrate his find. Kino names a list of things that he will secure for his family with his newfound wealth, including a church wedding and an education for his son. The neighbors marvel at Kino's boldness and wonder if he is foolish or wise to harbor such ambitions.

Toward evening, the local priest visits Kino to bless him in his good fortune and to remind him of his place within the church. Shortly thereafter, the doctor arrives, explaining that he was out in the morning but has come now to cure Coyotito. He administers a powdered capsule and promises to return in an hour.

In the intervening period, Coyotito grows violently ill, and Kino decides to bury the pearl under the floor in a corner of the brush house. The doctor returns and feeds Coyotito a potion to quiet his spasms. When the doctor inquires about payment, Kino explains that soon he will sell his large pearl and inadvertently glances toward the corner where he has hidden the pearl. This mention of the pearl greatly intrigues the doctor, and Kino is left with an uneasy feeling.

Before going to bed, Kino reburies the pearl under his sleeping mat. That night, he is roused by an intruder digging around in the corner. A violent struggle ensues, and Kino's efforts to chase away the criminal leave him bloodied. Terribly upset by this turn of events, Juana proposes that they abandon the pearl, which she considers an agent of evil.

The next morning, Kino and Juana make their way to town to sell the pearl. Juan Tomás, Kino's brother, advises Kino to be wary of cheats. Indeed, all of the dealers conspire to bid low on the pearl. Kino indignantly refuses to accept their offers, resolving instead to take his pearl to the capital. That evening, as Kino and Juana prepare to leave, Juan Tomás cautions Kino against being overly proud, and Juana repeats her wish to be rid of the pearl. Kino silences her, explaining that he is a man and will take care of things.

In the middle of the night, Juana steals away with the pearl. Kino wakes as she leaves and pursues her, apprehending her just as she is poised to throw the pearl into the sea. He tackles her, takes the pearl back, and beats her violently, leaving her in a crumpled heap on the beach. As he returns to the brush house, a group of hostile men confronts him and tries to take the pearl from him. He fights the men off, killing one and causing the rest to flee, but drops the pearl in the process.

As Juana ascends from the shore to the brush house, she finds the pearl lying in the path. Just beyond, she sees Kino on the ground, next to the dead man. He bemoans the loss of the pearl, which she presents to him. Though Kino explains that he had no intention to kill, Juana insists that he will be labeled a murderer. They resolve to flee at once. Kino rushes back to the shore to prepare the canoe, while Juana returns home to gather Coyotito and their belongings.

Kino arrives at the shore and finds his canoe destroyed by vandals. When he climbs the hill, he sees a fire blazing, and realizes that his house has burned down. Desperate to find refuge, Kino, Juana and Coyotito duck into Juan Tomás's house, where they hide out for the day. Relieved that the three did not perish in the blaze, as the rest of the neighborhood believes, Juan Tomás and his wife, Apolonia, reluctantly agree to keep Kino and Juana's secret and provide shelter for them while pretending to be ignorant of their whereabouts.

At nightfall, Kino, Juana, and Coyotito set out for the capital. Skirting the town, they travel north until sunrise and then take covert shelter by the roadside. They sleep for most of the day and are preparing to set out again when Kino discovers that three trackers are following them. After hesitating briefly, Kino decides that they must hurry up the mountain, in hopes of eluding the trackers. A breathless ascent brings them to a water source, where they rest and take shelter in a nearby cave. Kino attempts to mislead the trackers by creating a false trail up the mountain. Kino, Juana, and Coyotito then hide in the cave and wait for an opportunity to escape back down the mountain.

The trackers are slow in their pursuit and finally arrive at the watering hole at dusk. They make camp nearby, and two of the trackers sleep while the third stands watch. Kino decides that he must attempt to attack them before the late moon rises. He strips naked to avoid being seen and sneaks up to striking distance. Just as Kino prepares to attack, Coyotito lets out a cry, waking the sleepers. When one of them fires his rifle in the direction of the cry, Kino makes his move, killing the trackers in a violent fury. In the aftermath, Kino slowly realizes that the rifle shot struck and killed his son in the cave.

The next day, Kino and Juana make their way back through town and the outlying brush houses. Juana carries her dead son slung over her shoulder. They walk all the way to the sea, as onlookers watch in silent fascination. At the shore, Kino pulls the pearl out of his clothing and takes one last, hard look at it. Then, with all his might, under a setting sun, he flings the pearl back into the sea.

Character List

Kino   The protagonist of the novella. Kino is a dignified, hardworking, impoverished native who works as a pearl diver. He is a simple man who lives in a brush house with his wife, Juana, and their infant son, Coyotito, both of whom he loves very much. After Kino finds a great pearl, he becomes increasingly ambitious and desperate in his mission to break free of the oppression of his colonial society. Ultimately, Kino's material ambition drives him to a state of animalistic violence, and his life is reduced to a basic fight for survival.

Juana   Kino's young wife. After her prayers for good fortune in the form of a giant pearl are answered, Juana slowly becomes convinced that the pearl is in fact an agent of evil. Juana possesses a simple faith in divine powers, but she also thinks for herself. Unfortunately for her and her child, Coyotito, she subjects her desires to those of her dominant husband and allows Kino to hold on to the pearl.

Coyotito   Kino and Juana's only son, who is stung by a scorpion while resting in a hammock one morning. Because Coyotito is an infant, he is helpless to improve his situation and thus at the mercy of those who provide for him. Kino and Juana's efforts to save him by finding a big pearl with which they can pay a doctor prove to do more harm than good.

Juan Tomás   Kino's older brother. Deeply loyal to his family, Juan Tomás supports Kino in all of his endeavors but warns him of the dangers involved in possessing such a valuable pearl. He is sympathetic to Kino and Juana, however, putting them up when they need to hide and telling no one of their whereabouts.

Apolonia Juan Tomás's wife and the mother of four children. Like her husband, Apolonia is sympathetic to Kino and Juana's plight, and she agrees to give them shelter in their time of need.

The doctor A small-time colonial who dreams of returning to a bourgeois European lifestyle. The doctor initially refuses to treat Coyotito but changes his mind after learning that Kino has found a great pearl. He represents the arrogance, condescension, and greed at the heart of colonial society.

The priest The local village priest ostensibly represents moral virtue and goodness, but he is just as interested in exploiting Kino's wealth as everyone else, hoping that he can find a way to persuade Kino to give him some of the money he will make from the pearl.

The dealers The extremely well-organized and corrupt pearl dealers in La Paz systematically cheat and exploit the Indian pearl divers who sell them their goods. They desperately long to cheat Kino out of his pearl.

The trackers The group of violent and corrupt men that follows Kino and Juana when they leave the village, hoping to waylay Kino and steal his pearl.

ANALYSIS OF MAJOR CHARACTERS

KINO

Kino, *The Pearl*'s protagonist, is an extremely simple character, motivated by basic drives: his love for his family, loyalty to the traditions of his village and his people, and frustration at his people's oppression at the hands of their European colonizers. Kino also possesses a quick mind and a strong work ethic, and he feels a close, pure kinship with the natural world, the source of his livelihood.

At the beginning of the novella, Kino is essentially content with his life. However, two seemingly chance occurrences—Coyotito's scorpion sting and Kino's discovery of the pearl—open Kino's eyes to a larger world. As Kino begins to covet material wealth and education for his son, his simple existence becomes increasingly complicated by greed, conflict, and violence. The basic trajectory of Kino's character is a gradual decline from a state of innocence to a state of corruption and disillusionment. The forces propelling this decline are ambition and greed. At the end of the novella, Kino's tranquil relationship with nature has been perverted and reversed, a change signified by the fact that Kino finds the sounds of the animals at night threatening rather than reassuring.

Because *The Pearl* is a parable, Kino's character can be interpreted in many ways. It can be seen as a critique of colonial politics, an exploration of how good motives can bring a person to a bad end, or even an attack on the idea of the American dream. But on the most basic level, Kino represents the dangers of ambition and greed. Kino's ruin, caused by his lust for the pearl, illustrates the extent to which ambition and greed poison and jeopardize every aspect of a human's familial, cultural, and personal well-being.

JUANA

Kino's wife, Juana, is more reflective and more practical than Kino. She prays for divine aid when Coyotito's wound leaves Kino impotent with rage, and she also has the presence of mind to salve the wound with a seaweed poultice. Juana is loyal and submissive, obeying her husband as her culture dictates, but she does not always agree with his actions. Like Kino, Juana is at first seduced by the greed the pearl awakens, but she is much quicker than Kino to recognize the pearl as a potential threat. In fact, Juana comes to view the pearl as a symbol of evil.

As the novella progresses, Juana becomes certain that the limitations, rules, and customs of her society must be upheld. Whereas Kino seeks to transform his existence, Juana believes that their lives will be better if they keep things as they are. Kino can see only what they have to gain from the pearl, but Juana can see also what they stand to lose, and she wisely prefers to protect what she has rather than sacrifice it all for a dream. Juana thus serves an important function in the novella—she counterbalances Kino's enthusiasm and reminds the reader that Kino's desire to make money is dangerous. Juana also symbolizes the family's domestic happiness; the scene in which Kino beats her for trying to cast off the pearl thus represents Kino's tragic break from the family he longs to support.

The Doctor

Though he does not figure largely in the novella's plot, the doctor is an important character in *The Pearl* because he represents the colonial attitudes that oppress Kino's people. The doctor symbolizes and embodies the colonists' arrogance, greed, and condescension toward the natives, whom the colonists do not even try to understand. Like the other colonists, the doctor has no interest in Kino's people. He has come only to make money, and his greed distorts his human values. As a physician, the doctor is duty-bound to act to save human life, but when confronted with someone whom he considers beneath him, the doctor feels no such duty. His callous refusal to treat Coyotito for the scorpion sting because Kino lacks the money to pay him thus demonstrates the human cost of political conquest rooted in the desire for financial profit. As his interior monologue in Chapter 1 shows, the doctor is obsessed with European society, and European cultural values grip his mind so deeply that he doesn't even realize how ignorant he is of Kino and Kino's people.

Themes, Motifs & Symbols

Themes

Themes are the fundamental and often universal ideas explored in a literary work.

Greed as a Destructive Force

As Kino seeks to gain wealth and status through the pearl, he transforms from a happy, contented father to a savage criminal, demonstrating the way ambition and greed destroy innocence. Kino's desire to acquire wealth perverts the pearl's natural beauty and good luck, transforming it from a symbol of hope to a symbol of human destruction. Furthermore, Kino's greed leads him to behave violently toward his wife; it also leads to his son's death and ultimately to Kino's detachment from his cultural traditions and his society. Kino's people seem poised for a similar destruction, as the materialism inherent in colonial capitalism implants a love of profit into the simple piety of the native people.

The Roles of Fate and Agency in Shaping Human Life

The Pearl portrays two contrasting forces that shape human life and determine individual destiny. The novella depicts a world in which, for the most part, humans shape their own destinies. They provide for themselves, follow their own desires, and make their own plans. At the same time, forces beyond human control, such as chance, accident, and the gods, can sweep in at any moment and, for good or ill, completely change the course of an individual's life. If fate is best represented in the novella by the open sea where pearl divers plunge beneath the waves hoping for divine blessings, human agency is best represented by the village of La Paz, where myriad human desires, plans, and motives come together to form civilization.

Kino and Juana's lives change irreparably the moment the scorpion, a symbol of malignant fate, bites their child. Their lives then change irreparably again the moment Kino finds the pearl, a symbol of beneficent fate. Nevertheless, it is not fate but human agency, in the form of greed, ambition, and violence, that facilitates the novella's disastrous final outcome, as Kino's greed and the greed of others lead to a series of conflicts over the pearl. Kino finds himself caught between the forces of fate and the forces of human society, between the destiny handed him by fate and the destiny he seeks to create himself.

Colonial Society's Oppression of Native Cultures

The doctor who refuses to save Coyotito's life at the beginning of the novel because Kino lacks the money to pay him represents colonial arrogance and oppression. Snide and condescending, the doctor displays an appallingly limited and self-centered mind-set that is made frightening by his unshakable belief in his own cultural superiority over Kino, and by the power that he holds to save or destroy lives. Steinbeck implicitly accuses the doctor's entire colonial society of such destructive arrogance, greed, and ambition. The European colonizers that govern Kino and the native people are shown to bring about the destruction of the native society's innocence, piety, and purity.

Motifs

Motifs are recurring structures, contrasts, and literary devices that can help to develop and inform the text's major themes.

Nature Imagery

Kino's physical and spiritual existence is intimately connected with the natural world. He lives in a brush house, and he makes his living as a pearl diver. Not surprisingly, nature imagery is an important element of the novella. Kino observes the world of his garden in the opening scene of Chapter 1 and the world of the ocean in Chapter 2. Kino and Juana's final journey up the mountain takes place on a dark night full of animal noises and cries.

Steinbeck depicts the natural world as a realm that mirrors or parallels the human world. Overall, the work's nature imagery reflects both the natural world's idyllic innocence—the innocence Kino possesses at the beginning of the novella—and the natural world's darker qualities of struggle and flight—the struggle and flight Kino experiences at the novella's end. *The Pearl*'s descriptions of the sea, for instance, subtly emphasize the fact that life in the sea is a struggle for survival from which only the strongest emerge alive—a struggle that mirrors the conflict between Kino and the native people against their colonial rulers. Kino's two interactions with ants—the first in Chapter 1, the second in Chapter 6—create a parallel between Kino's relationship to nature and the gods' relationship to Kino (he towers over the ants in the same way that the gods tower over him).

Kino's Songs

Throughout the novel, whenever Kino has a particularly powerful feeling or instinct, he hears a song in his head that corresponds to that feeling. When he is happy with his family in Chapter 1, for instance, he hears the Song of the Family. When he senses malice or dishonesty, he hears the Song of Evil. These songs point to the oral nature of Kino's cultural tradition. The ancient, familiar songs, presumably handed down from generation to generation, occupy such a central place in how Kino's people perceive themselves that the songs actually give form to their inner feelings. Kino is much less likely to become aware of the sensation of wariness than he is to hear the Song of Danger in his head. Similarly, he is much less likely to take action because of his own conscious judgment than because he associates the song with a certain kind of urgent behavior in relation to the outside world. The songs also point to Steinbeck's original conception of *The Pearl* as a film project; in a motion picture, the songs could be played out loud for the audience to hear and thus function as recurring motifs and melodies that would underscore the story's themes.

Symbols

Symbols are objects, characters, figures, and colors used to represent abstract ideas or concepts.

The Pearl

Because *The Pearl* is a parable, the meaning of the pearl itself—the novella's central symbol—is never explicitly defined. Nevertheless, though the nature of the pearl's symbolism is left to each reader's interpretation, this symbolism seems to shift over the course of the work. At first, the pearl represents a stroke of divine providence. Kino's people have a prophecy about a great "Pearl That Might Be," a perfect pearl that exists as a perfect possibility. Kino and Juana's discovery of the pearl seems to fulfill this prophecy, and it fills them with hope for Coyotito's future and for the possibility of a life free from the shackles of colonial oppression. The discovery of the pearl seems a happy accident, one that counterbalances the tragic accident of Coyotito's scorpion sting.

Once the town finds out about the pearl, however, the object begins to make everyone who beholds it, including Kino, greedy. The neighbors call it "the Pearl of the World," and while that title originally seems to refer to the pearl's great size and beauty, it also underscores the fact that having the pearl brings the outside world's destructive influence into Kino's simple life. As the dealers begin lowballing him, Kino ceases to view the pearl with optimistic delight and instead focuses on its sale with determined ambition. The pearl's association with good fortune and hope weakens, and the pearl becomes associated more strongly with human plans and desires. Juana and Juan Tomás begin to view the pearl as a threat rather than a blessing.

The pearl elicits more and more greed on Kino's part, as he begins to devote all his energies and possessions to protecting it (recalling the biblical parable of the pearl of great price). It thus comes to symbolize the destructive nature of materialism. The implication is that Kino's acquisition of material wealth isn't enough to save him from the colonists' oppression, even though such wealth is the foundation of the colonists' capitalist system. In fact, Kino's shift in focus from his spiritual well-being to his material status seems to represent the colonists' ultimate triumph.

The way the pearl is depicted through the course of the novella mirrors the changes that Kino himself undergoes. At first, the pearl is a simple and beautiful object of nature. Once it becomes entangled with notions of material value, however, it becomes destructive and dangerous. The pearl is an object of natural beauty and goodness that draws out the evil inherent in mankind.

The Scorpion

The scorpion that stings Coyotito in Chapter 1 symbolizes a seemingly arbitrary evil that, because it has nothing to do with human agency, must come from the gods. Biblically, the scorpion generally represents the destruction of innocence, and the fact that Coyotito is a baby compounds the Christian symbolism of the event. Coyotito is touched by evil, and this natural destruction of innocence repeats itself in the novella in the destruction of Kino's innocence by his ambition and greed and in the destruction of the natives' traditional, natural way of life by the colonists.

Kino's Canoe

A means of making a living—both pearls and food—that has been passed down for generations, the canoe that Kino uses represents his link to cultural tradition. This culture is deeply spiritual, so it is significant that Kino uses the canoe to find the pearl, which is provided by a divine power that has nothing to do with human agency. It is also significant that Kino's possession of the pearl leads directly to the canoe's destruction, in Chapter 5, an event that symbolizes Kino's devastating decision to break with his cultural heritage because he wishes to pursue material gain.

Parable & the Form of *The Pearl*

> *"If this story is a parable, perhaps everyone takes his own meaning from it and reads his own life into it."*
> (See QUOTATIONS, p. 41)

A parable is a simple story that relays a moral lesson. Frequently, parables are also allegories, stories in which characters, objects, and events hold fixed symbolic meaning. Steinbeck's focus on the symbolic role the pearl plays in Kino's life is constant, as is his focus on the symbolic importance of Kino himself. In general, Steinbeck's overly simplistic portrayal of events is not realistic, or even believable, and it indicates *The Pearl*'s place as a parable or fable.

Kino is an impoverished native fisherman, but more important is his allegorical role as a man faced with the temptation of wealth beyond his wildest dreams. Because the novella is concerned with Kino's moral obligation and not his civic obligation, it concludes with Kino's casting the pearl back into the sea, a renunciation of material wealth that indicates he has learned a moral lesson. It is important that the novella does not conclude with Kino's arrest or continuing flight from justice, as a realistic novel concerned with civic punishment for ethical transgression might.

Despite the apparent gulf between realism and parable, *The Pearl* attempts to show how the two are linked through the process of storytelling. Steinbeck suggests that a culture's collective memory eventually fictionalizes all realistic experience into parable form. "As with all retold tales that are in people's hearts," he writes in the novella's epigraph, "there are only good and bad things and black and white things and good and evil things and no in-between anywhere." Storytelling gradually transforms real occurrences into simplified parables designed to teach a specific lesson. While everyday life may lack a clear lesson or meaning, the human mind is always in the process of ordering and classifying events in order to make sense of experience. It is a human tendency, and therefore a literary tendency, to classify and simplify experience, to turn reality into parable.

As codified systems of morals that attempt to distinguish good from evil, religions depend heavily on parables. According to the New Testament, Jesus himself insisted on teaching to his disciples in parable form—in fact, the Christian parable of the pearl of great price, which tells the story of a man who gives up everything he has to win a great pearl, likely helped to inspire *The Pearl*. Steinbeck realizes that the parable form is a central element in world religion and in the cultural history of humankind. As *The Pearl* illustrates, the imagined is just as vital to humankind's understanding of life as the real, and, in the form of the parable, the two are inextricably linked.

Although readers may draw a number of messages from *The Pearl*, a few primary moral lessons do emerge. Some ways of interpreting the allegory of the story include:

THE STRUGGLE TO PRESERVE VIRTUE
If the pearl symbolizes goodness, Kino's struggle to protect the cherished pearl might represent the human struggle to preserve cherished qualities or attributes—moral virtue, innocence, integrity, the soul—from the destructive forces of the outside world. Just as these destructive forces corrupt and conspire to seize Kino's pearl, they can work against the virtuous inner qualities that the pearl might represent. According to this reading, Coyotito's death and Kino's voluntary relinquishment of the pearl at the end of the novel suggest that the destructive forces of the world are too powerful to be overcome.

THE FALLACY OF THE AMERICAN DREAM
In a way, Kino's desire to use the pearl to improve his life echoes the traditional narrative of the American dream. He attempts to transform hard work into material wealth, and material wealth into education, comfort, and familial advancement. According to this reading, Kino's gradual corruption and the story's tragic conclusion hint at a fundamental flaw in the American dream: it condones sacrifice of virtue for material gain. Additionally, Kino's gradual disillusionment with the pearl (as he realizes that it won't make his life better) underscores the fallacy of the American dream itself. Rather than widespread opportunity, Kino finds a world of powerful, greedy men conniving to take his wealth away from him dishonestly.

The Effects of Colonialism on Native Cultures

Because Kino belongs to a native tribe that, centuries after the original Spanish colonization of Mexico, is still under the thumb of the Spanish colonial authorities, the story can be read as a parable about the forces of colonization and the destructive effect those forces have on native cultures and peoples. Kino is originally driven to search for the pearl because of the unhelpfulness of the condescending Spanish doctor; after he finds the pearl, he is cheated and hunted by cynical descendants of colonials who hope to exploit and control him.

Greed Is the Root of All Evil

This moral, preached by St. Augustine and many others after him, is found in the New Testament in Paul's first epistle to Timothy (1 Timothy 6:10). Kino's investment of spiritual value in a pearl, an object of material wealth, may be misguided from the start. Juana and Juan Tomás both suspect that Kino is wrong to try to get more for the pearl than the dealers offer, and Juana tries several times to discard the pearl, believing it to be the source of her family's troubles. This reading interprets the pearl as a symbol of destruction and corruption rather than purity.

Summary & Analysis

Chapter 1

Summary

> *Kino watched with the detachment of God while a dusty ant frantically tried to escape the sand trap an ant lion had dug for him.*
>
> *(See* QUOTATIONS, *p. 41)*

Just before sunrise sometime around 1900, a Mexican-Indian pearl diver named Kino awakens to the sound of crowing roosters. He lives near the village of La Paz, on the Pacific coast of the Baja Peninsula. He watches the day dawning through the crack of the door to his house, which is made of brush—bundles of straw fastened together to form walls and a roof. He then looks to a makeshift cradle, a kind of box hanging from the roof of the hut, where his infant son, Coyotito, sleeps. Finally, still resting on the mat, Kino turns his gaze to the open eyes of his wife, Juana. She looks back at Kino as she always does in the early morning. Hearing the waves rolling up on the nearby beach, Kino closes his eyes again to listen to the sound of an old song in his head.

Juana rises to check on Coyotito and starts a fire. Kino also rises, wrapping himself in a blanket and sliding into his sandals. Outside, he regards the climbing sun and the hovering clouds as Juana prepares breakfast. In the company of a goat and a dog, Kino stares "with the detachment of God" at a group of industrious ants underfoot. Behind him, Kino hears Juana singing and nursing Coyotito. Her song is simple, and it moves Kino to contemplation.

As the rest of the neighborhood stirs, Kino goes back inside the house and finds Juana fixing her hair. As they eat their simple breakfast, there is no speech between them beyond a contented sigh from Kino. A ray of light shines on Coyotito's hanging box, revealing a scorpion crawling down the rope toward the child. Terrified, Juana recites a charm and a prayer to protect Coyotito, while Kino moves forward to capture the scorpion.

Coyotito spots the scorpion on the rope, laughs, and reaches up to grab it. Just then, positioned in front of the hanging box, Kino freezes, slowly stretching out his hand toward the scorpion. When Coyotito shakes the rope of the hanging box, the scorpion falls, lands on his shoulder, and stings him. Kino immediately seizes the creature and crushes it in his grasp, beating it to death on the floor for good measure. Kino's retribution does no good, though, and Coyotito screams with pain.

Juana grabs Coyotito at once and attempts to suck the venom out of his festering wound. The child's wailing summons several neighbors to Kino's doorstep, including Kino's brother, Juan Tomás, and Juan Tomás's wife, Apolonia. As Coyotito's cries diminish into moans, Juana asks Kino to summon the doctor. Such a request surprises the neighbors since the doctor has never visited the poor cluster of brush houses. (The doctor belongs to the social class of the Spanish colonists of the region, a class far above that of poor natives such as Kino and Juana.) When Kino expresses doubt that the doctor will come to Coyotito, Juana resolves to take Coyotito to the doctor. Kino and Juana set out for the center of town, their neighbors trailing behind them.

Near the center of town, more people follow, curious to see the outcome of a poor man's plea to a rich doctor. Arriving at the doctor's house, Kino knocks at the gate. He both fears and resents the doctor, a powerful man not of his own people. Presently, the gate opens to reveal one of Kino's own people, employed in the doctor's service. Kino explains the details of Coyotito's injury in his native tongue; the man ignores Kino's use of the native language and responds in Spanish. He tells Kino to wait while he goes to speak with the doctor.

Indoors, the doctor sits up in bed, surrounded by luxuries. He feasts on biscuits and hot chocolate and thinks nostalgically of Paris. When the servant interrupts the doctor's reverie to announce Kino's visit, the doctor bitterly demands to know if Kino has money to pay for the treatment. Kino gives the servant eight small pearls, but soon the servant returns to Kino with them, explaining that the doctor has been called out to attend to a serious case. With this dismissal, the procession breaks up, leaving Kino furious and ashamed. Standing in shock in front of the closed gate, Kino strikes out in anger, smashing his fist into the barrier and bloodying his knuckles.

Analysis

As its short, simple sentences and heavily symbolic moral overtones make evident, *The Pearl* is based on the form of biblical parable, and the simple natural beauty of the opening scene recalls the beauty and innocence of the Garden of Eden before Adam and Eve's fall. Though the comparison is not made explicitly, it is nevertheless an apt one—like Adam and Eve, Kino and Juana make choices later in the story that cause them to lose their innocence and force them to leave their paradise for the hardships of the wider world. The cluster of brush houses by the sea where Kino and Juana live functions as a kind of paradise, in which man and woman live together in a state of nature. Steinbeck focuses on the family's rustic simplicity and on its reverence for a higher power. Steinbeck uses repetitious language, which evokes the Bible and other religious literature, to underscore the family's spirituality. This scriptural structure is especially evident in Steinbeck's frequent use of the word "and" to drive the narrative: "And a goat came near and sniffed at him"; "And the rhythm of the family song was the grinding stone"; "And he drank a little pulque and that was breakfast."

Kino's knowledge of the world is not expansive, but his store of traditional songs and his contented, familiar manner of surveying his meager territory show that he is intimately acquainted with every aspect of the existence he knows. Kino frequently hears traditional songs in his head that express his mood or his sense of his environment—when he is content at home in this chapter, he hears the soothing rhythms of the Song of the Family, for instance, but when he is in trouble later in the novella he hears the alarming Song of Danger. Kino's inner soundtrack highlights *The Pearl*'s original conception as a film project—the audience would actually have heard these songs and experienced them as recurring motifs. It also points to the oral nature of Kino's culture, in which songs are passed down from generation to generation and assume such a position of psychological importance that they actually provide an internal context without which Kino is unable to interpret his own feelings.

Steinbeck seems to suggest that the imminent disruption of Kino's Eden, like the harmony that precedes it, is the work of a divine power. Like Kino, who observes the ants as though he were a detached God, the God watching over Kino—and indeed all humanity in the text—shows indifference to the cruel combination of successes and failures that people encounter. As Kino surveys the surroundings of his brush house, wild doves fly and ruffled roosters fight, symbolizing the way good and evil haphazardly commingle.

The scorpion that brings terror into Kino's household represents the work of a divine agent. In Christian literature, scorpions traditionally symbolize evil, and the streak of sunlight that falls on the scorpion as it rests on the hanging box rope seems a heavenly spotlight, setting the drama in motion. With the Song of Evil drowning out the Song of Family, Kino must take control of his family's destiny after this unkind twist of fate.

Steinbeck's writing evinces contempt for the town doctor, who surrounds himself with the vulgar trappings of European "civilized living." To Steinbeck, the doctor's notion of civilization is utterly materialistic and devoid of the complex spirituality so integral to Kino and Juana's life. Nevertheless, the doctor's barbaric beliefs hold sway in this colonial context, and the divide between rich and poor seems racially and inflexibly defined.

The doctor's servant, as a native employed by a colonial, demonstrates the divide between the world of the doctor that of Kino and Juana. The servant is overly official and speaks Spanish when receiving Kino and Juana, underscoring the social differences between Kino and the doctor. He does, however, revert to their native language in a more sympathetic moment. While the servant possesses the capacity to move—linguistically and otherwise—between two disparate worlds, the colonial doctor possesses neither the linguistic ability nor the desire to do so. Though Kino desires to cross between the two worlds too, he is unable to do so. This powerlessness renders his indignation at the doctor's refusal to treat Coyotito irrelevant, since he has no productive means to express this indignation.

CHAPTER 2

SUMMARY

> *But the pearls were accidents, and the finding of one was luck, a little pat on the back by God or the gods or both.*
>
> (See QUOTATIONS, p. 43)

On the shores of the estuary, a set of blue and white canoes sits in the sand. Crabs and lobsters poke out from their holes, and algae and sea horses drift aimlessly in the nearby currents. Dogs and pigs scavenge the shoreline for sea drift in the hazy morning. Amid this scene, Kino and Juana walk down the beach to Kino's canoe. They are going to search for pearls, desperately hoping to find a pearl of sufficient value to persuade the doctor to treat the poisoned Coyotito.

The canoe, an heirloom passed down to Kino from his paternal grandfather, is Kino's sole asset in the world. Kino lays his blanket in its bow. Juana rests Coyotito upon the blanket and places her shawl over him to protect him from the sun. She then wades into the water and collects some seaweed, which she applies gently to Coyotito's wound.

Kino and Juana slide the canoe into the water, Juana climbs in, and Kino pushes the boat away from shore. Once Kino boards, the two begin paddling out to sea in search of pearls. In a short time, they come upon other canoes, which have clustered around the nearest oyster bed. Kino makes a dive to collect oysters, while Juana stays in the canoe, praying for luck. He stays under water for over two minutes, gathering the largest shells, including one especially enormous oyster that has a "ghostly gleam."

Climbing back into the canoe, Kino is reluctant to examine the largest oyster first. After halfheartedly pawing at a smaller one, eagerness overcomes him, and Juana softly urges him to open the prize catch. Kino cuts the shell open to reveal the biggest pearl that either of them has ever seen. Nearly breathless, Juana shrieks in astonishment to find that Coyotito's wound has improved in the presence of the great pearl. Kino, overcome with emotion, tenses his entire body and lets out a resounding yell. Startled by this unexpected display, the other canoes quickly race toward Kino and Juana to uncover the source of the commotion.

Analysis

Steinbeck writes that for those natives who live by the estuary, at the edge of earth, sea, and sky, "there was . . . no proof that what you saw was there or was not there." He emphasizes the vast, hazy nature of the surrounding landscape to depict the natives as a caste of natural visionaries. Despite their lack of scientific knowledge gained through observation, the natives of the brush houses understand the world because they trust what Steinbeck calls "things of the spirit."

Such an unscientific approach to life contrasts starkly with the pragmatic, rationalist approach that colonial society imposes upon the gulf—the approach to life that the doctor exemplifies. It also contrasts with the materialistic approach of the American audience to whom Steinbeck addresses his work. Steinbeck renders this contrast in a subtle manner, by placing more value on Juana's care and intuition in her treatment of Coyotito's wound than on the training and apparent wealth of the callous doctor. Though Juana's improvised seaweed poultice works as well or better for her stricken son than a doctor's treatment, it lacks authority because of its unscientific simplicity. This respect for tradition and simple piety above the material and technological trappings of industrial society persists throughout the novella.

The narrator reveals the natives' willingness to accept both old and new belief systems when he asserts that "the finding of [a pearl] was luck, a little pat on the back by God or the gods, or both." Juana's willingness to appeal to anything that works—monotheism, polytheism, superstition—exemplifies this religious ambivalence. When Juana prays as Kino dives into the sea to search for pearls, her faith in "things of the spirit" is further revealed to be incomplete. Instead of praying for Coyotito to heal magically, which seems an impossible occurrence, Juana prays for Kino to find a pearl large enough to pay for the doctor's services, an occurrence that is only improbable. Juana's prayer suggests a belief not in divine miracles but in luck. It also shows her acceptance of, or defeat by, the capitalist system—she wishes for a pearl that will provide the means to *purchase* the healing powers of a doctor. By intimating that one should ask directly for what one wants, Steinbeck portrays Juana's indirect appeal as foolish. His intention is not to patronize the natives but rather to suggest the shortsightedness of all people.

The "ghostly gleam" of the oyster that bears the unusually large pearl suggests the pearl's extraordinary significance and supernatural quality. Clearly, this pearl is unlike any other; it seems as though fate (and, of course, Steinbeck himself) has placed it in Kino's hands in his most desperate hour. Steinbeck thus positions the pearl to be the focal point for the development of Kino's character over the course of the novella.

Chapter 3

Summary

> *My son will read and open the books . . . he will know and through him we will know. . . . This is what the pearl will do.*
>
> (See QUOTATIONS, p. 44)

Word of Kino's discovery travels quickly. Even before Kino returns to his brush house, everyone in town knows that he has found "the Pearl of the World." Throughout town, people of every class—from the beggar to the businessman to the priest—dream of how Kino's pearl can help them. Like everyone else, the doctor who turned Kino away desires the pearl.

Ignorant of others' jealousy, Kino and Juana delight in their good fortune, inviting family and friends to share their joy in their newfound treasure. When Juan Tomás asks Kino what he will do with his wealth, Kino details his plans: a proper marriage in the church, new clothing for the family, a harpoon, and a rifle, among other things. Kino's new boldness amazes Juana, especially when he expresses his desire for Coyotito to be sent to school and educated. Kino himself is surprised somewhat by his own resolute statement, and all of the neighbors stare at the mighty pearl with a mixture of hope and fear at the enormous changes that lie ahead.

As dusk approaches, Juana revives the fire, and the neighbors overstay their welcome. Near dark, the priest comes to deliver a benediction. Once he has blessed the household, he asks to see the pearl. Dazzled, the priest implores Kino to remember the church in his new prosperity. Juana announces their intention to be married in the church, and the priest leaves them with a kind word. A sense of evil overcomes Kino in the wake of the priest's visit.

The neighbors disperse to their own suppers, and Juana begins to prepare a meal of baked beans. Kino huddles beneath a blanket in the cold night, keeping the pearl close to his body. Plagued with continued ill feeling, Kino meditates on the former security of his family, and on the menacing uncertainty into which their newfound fortune has cast them.

From the door of his brush house, Kino watches two men approach. The figures prove to be the doctor and his servant, who have come to examine Coyotito's wound. Kino brusquely dismisses the doctor's attentions, but when the doctor makes a sinister insinuation about the lingering potential for infection, Kino relents and allows him to enter. Juana is extremely suspicious of the doctor, but Kino reassures her. When the doctor examines Coyotito, he contends that he has found evidence of complications and produces a capsule of medication that he proceeds to administer. Claiming that the poison will strike within an hour and that the medicine may prove lifesaving, the doctor declares that he will return in an hour to check on Coyotito's progress.

As Juana stares at Coyotito with concern, Kino realizes that he has been careless in not guarding the pearl. Without delay, he wraps the pearl in a rag, digs a hole, and buries the pearl in a corner of the brush house, concealing the hiding place from view. As Kino eats his supper, a small black puppy lingers in the doorway and shakes its tail nervously. Afterward, Juana alerts Kino that Coyotito's condition is growing worse, and she sings soothingly in an effort to comfort the baby. When Coyotito becomes visibly ill, an evil feeling fills Kino once again.

The neighbors learn quickly of the doctor's visit and Coyotito's subsequent decline, and they reconvene at Kino's house to provide support. The doctor reappears, and a swiftly administered potion sets Coyotito to rest. The doctor innocuously asks when Kino might be able to pay him. Kino explains that once he has sold his most valuable pearl he will be able to pay.

Feigning ignorance about the pearl, the doctor offers to keep it in his safe, but Kino declines the offer, explaining that he intends to sell the pearl in the morning. The doctor expresses concern that the pearl might be stolen, and Kino inadvertently glances with fear at the corner where the pearl is buried. Later, when the doctor and neighbors depart and it is time to sleep, Kino paces about the house anxiously, listening vigilantly for threatening noises. In a fit of precaution, he digs up the pearl and reburies it beneath his sleeping mat. Finally, Kino, Juana, and Coyotito curl up together on the mat and attempt to sleep peacefully.

At first, Kino dreams of Coyotito's future success, but the evil feeling returns and quickly overtakes him. He stirs restlessly, waking Juana. He wakes and hears an intruder in the house, cowering and scratching in the corner, clearly in search of the pearl. Grabbing his knife, Kino leaps into the corner and struggles with the intruder, stabbing at him wildly. After a violent scuffle, the intruder flees, leaving Kino bloodied as Juana calls out to him in terror. Regaining her senses, she swiftly prepares a salve for Kino's bruised forehead.

As she tends Kino's wounds, Juana rails against the pearl, calling it an evil plague upon them. Kino remains adamant about the pearl's virtue, insisting that it will be their road to salvation. Juana disagrees, declaring that it will destroy their entire family. As Kino hushes her, he notices a spot of blood on his knife, which he removes. With dawn approaching, he settles down to look at his pearl. In its luminescence, Kino sees his family's chance for the future, and smiles. Juana smiles with him, and they meet the day with hope.

Analysis

Though *The Pearl*'s narrative seems to suggest that greed is the first step to destruction, in this chapter Steinbeck focuses not on greed but on ambition—Kino's desire to use the wealth offered by the pearl to better his life and the life of his family. Steinbeck portrays this kind of benevolent desire for advancement as a trait unique to humanity, one that has made humankind superior to all animals. Kino's neighbors have trouble figuring whether Kino's ambition will bring him success or suffering. They too are intoxicated by the awe-inspiring prospect of Kino owning a rifle or Coyotito receiving an education, but these propositions are so far removed from their sense of what is possible that they react to them with a natural suspicion. The neighbors are only able to think about the pearl in terms of their preexisting narratives. Because they have an ancient legend about a great "Pearl That Might Be," they believe that that legend has come to fruition in Kino's pearl, which they dub the "Pearl of the World." They do not conceive of the pearl as simply a valuable lucky break for Kino; for them, the pearl has deep moral and spiritual significance. By relating the stories the neighbors trade, Steinbeck shows how the human mind turns real experience into parable through the act of storytelling.

For us, the neighbors' suspicion of Kino's good fortune seems justified, based on Steinbeck's tentative tone and on his remarks that the gods disregard men's plans and only allow men success if it comes by accident. Steinbeck asserts that when human agency actually does bring about success (through the exercise of a benevolent ambition like Kino's, for example), "the gods take their revenge on a man." In this way, Steinbeck completely negates the value system of the American dream. Hard work and openness to opportunity, the main components of the traditional American dream, are meaningless in a malevolent universe in which "the gods" conspire against every individual's desire to improve his or her lot in life.

Because his pearl is worth so much money, Kino believes it offers him a chance to realize his ambitious dreams and free himself from the shackles of colonialism. But what keeps Kino from fulfilling his ambitions is his lack of knowledge. Kino may be able to pay the doctor to heal his son, but he is ignorant as to whether he is making the right choice—perhaps the doctor is in fact poisoning his son. Kino is well aware of his predicament, and his desire for his son to obtain an education shows Kino's recognition that education provides the only possible escape from colonial oppression. But in his single-minded pursuit of success and wealth for his son, Kino abandons the nurturing aspects of his fatherly duty. Kino leaves Juana alone to care for the ailing Coyotito while he, Kino, focuses his attentions on finding a place to conceal the pearl.

As Kino shifts his focus to providing for his son in material rather than emotional ways, he makes a corresponding shift from peaceful coexistence in his village to violent, paranoid suspicion of his neighbors. Now that Kino has acquired wealth, he is obligated to defend that wealth from potential usurpers. Ultimately, this shift in preoccupation demonstrates that wealth has a dehumanizing effect on those who possess it, such as the doctor and Kino, and on those who desire it, such as the intruder who comes to steal the pearl. The intruder is described in vague, inhuman terms that portray him as an unidentifiable mass of clothing. Kino even refers to him as "the thing," as though he were a plague sent against Kino rather than another human being. At this point in the story, however, only Juana seems to recognize that the pearl is an evil instrument that will bring her family pain and heartache.

CHAPTER 4

SUMMARY

Word spreads throughout the town of La Paz that Kino will be selling his great pearl. The pearl buyers are especially excited, and the pearl fishers abandon their work for the day to witness the transaction. Over breakfast that morning, the brush-house neighborhood teems with speculation and opinion. Kino, Juana, and Coyotito wear their best clothes for the occasion, and Kino dons his hat with care, anxious to appear a serious, vigorous man of the world.

As Kino and Juana set out from their brush house, the neighbors fall in line behind them. Juan Tomás walks at the front with Kino and expresses his concern that Kino may be cheated, as Kino has no standard of true comparison to know what his pearl is worth. Kino acknowledges this problem but adds that they have no way of solving it. Juan Tomás tells Kino that another system of pearl-selling used to exist before Kino was born. Pearlers would give their pearls to agents for sale in the capital, but as a result of the rampant corruption of pearl agents who stole the pearls meant for sale, the old system is no longer in place. Kino points out that according to the church, such a system must fail, as it represents a vain effort on the part of the pearlers to exceed their station in life.

Kino and Juan Tomás walk on in silence into the city, drawing stares from assembled onlookers. As Kino, Juan Tomás, and the attending crowd approach, the pearl dealers scramble to put their offices in order, hiding their little pearls and preparing to make offers. The first dealer is a short, slick man who nervously rolls a coin back and forth in his hand. He explains after a careful examination that the pearl is worthless because of its abnormally large size. Declaring it more of a museum curiosity than a market commodity, the dealer makes an offhand bid of one thousand pesos.

Kino reacts angrily to this lowball offer and insists that the pearl is worth fifty times that much. The dealer firmly asserts that his is an accurate appraisal and invites Kino to seek out a second opinion. Kino's neighbors stir uneasily, wondering how Kino can reject such a large sum of money and wondering whether he is being foolish and headstrong by demanding more. Presently, three new dealers arrive to examine the pearl, and the initial dealer invites them to make independent appraisals.

The first two dealers reject the pearl as a mere oddity, and the third dealer makes a feeble offer of five hundred pesos. Upon hearing this news, Kino quickly removes the pearl from consideration. As he does so, the initial dealer, unfazed by the lower bid, insists that his offer of one thousand pesos still stands. Protesting that he has been cheated, Kino announces a plan to sell his pearl in the capital city. His outburst raises the bid to fifteen hundred pesos, but Kino will have none of it. He fiercely pushes his way out of the crowd and starts the long walk home as Juana trails after him.

At supper, Kino's neighbors debate the day's events. Some suggest that the dealers' appraisals were fair, while others think that Kino is the victim of a scam. Some think he should have settled for the final offer of fifteen hundred pesos; others praise Kino's bravery for insisting on his own terms.

Meanwhile, in his brush house, Kino has buried the pearl under his sleeping mat. He sits brooding, nervous about his upcoming journey to the faraway capital. Juana watches him while she nurses Coyotito and prepares supper. Juan Tomás then enters to try to warn Kino of the dangers involved in going to the capital, but Kino is adamant about selling his pearl to secure a better future for his son. Unable to convince Kino to heed his warning, Juan Tomás returns home.

That night Kino goes without supper. He sits awake to protect the pearl and continues to pore over the details of his problem. Juana keeps her own silent vigil, intending to support Kino with her company. Suddenly, Kino senses an evil presence. He rises, feeling for the knife under his shirt, and moves toward the doorway as Juana stifles a desire to restrain him. From the darkness, a man assaults Kino, and a struggle ensues. By the time Juana reaches the fray, the attacker has fled. Bloodied and cut and with his clothes torn, Kino lies sprawled on the ground, only half conscious.

Without delay, Juana helps Kino inside to care for his wounds. Kino admits that in the dark he was unable to tell who attacked him. After Juana washes out his last cut, she begs him in desperation to discard the evil pearl. But, more fiercely than ever, Kino insists that they must capitalize on their good fortune. He explains that in the morning they will set out in the canoe for the capital. Juana dutifully submits to her husband's plan, and they both go to sleep.

Analysis

Like Chapter 3, Chapter 4 opens with a comment by the narrator about the town—"It is wonderful the way a little town keeps track of itself and of all its units." Steinbeck goes on to portray the town as an all-powerful unit, full of men who work together to suppress the deviant elements in their midst. Steinbeck emphasizes that society shapes an individual's fate as much as divinity or any other force. In the universe of *The Pearl*, the gods assert their influence on humans through chance and accident, but society asserts an equal influence through forces—such as greed and violence—that emanate from human drives. Both human will and the gods shape Kino's fate in Steinbeck's parable: an accident enables Kino to find the pearl, and greed and ambition lead to his downfall.

The narrator says that peace can be achieved in the town only if no one deviates from normal, expected behavior, implying that towns are almost like miniature authoritarian states. It is ironic that Steinbeck names the town in *The Pearl* La Paz, which means "peace" in Spanish. The town's capitalist cartel wages constant war with all challengers, and by possessing a great pearl, Kino makes himself a target for the racket of pearl buyers that has evolved over time. Behind the scenes, one man determines how much the buyers should offer for each pearl, thereby profiting shamelessly while remaining out of the reach of accusation. An individual selling a pearl therefore has no alternative but to comply with this system or, despite the difficulty of doing so, try to circumvent it.

Kino's comment to Juan Tomás that the old system of pearl selling was "against religion" highlights the way the Catholic church preserved existing social hierarchies and gross disparities in wealth by cautioning its followers about the relative unimportance and even danger of the material world. The narrator adds that the natives of Mexico have endured this position at the bottom of the social hierarchy, including its absolute and total exploitation of both financial and moral terms, for the four hundred years since the first Europeans arrived.

The thieflike pearl dealers Kino encounters lack names, character complexity, and emotion—they seem to lack humanity. A profit margin dictates their entire existence, and their livelihoods depend upon underhanded deals, as symbolized by the fact that the first dealer spends all his time secretly practicing a coin trick beneath his desk. When one neighbor asks if the dealers conspired in advance regarding the price of the pearl, another neighbor responds, "If that is so, then all of us have been cheated all of our lives." It is almost as though such a possibility is too horrible to for the natives to face. Instead, everyone chooses to ignore the legitimacy of the suggestion, and most of the villagers ridicule Kino's defiance of the dealers.

While we sympathize with Kino's desire to break free from oppression (as Juan Tomás realizes, Kino's ambition pits him against an entire established structure of business, church, and empire), Kino's treatment of Juana lessens our sympathy for him somewhat. Juana finds herself subjected to Kino's whims just as he is subjected to the colonists' whims. She has no role in the business process, and Kino never consults her about the proper course of action with regard to the pearl. When Juana finally volunteers her intuition that the pearl is evil and will ruin them, Kino refuses to listen, assuring her with the simple declaration "I am a man." Juana has no recourse. Kino's refusal to acknowledge his wife's better judgment parallels the colonial suppression of the native's intuitive knowledge of "things of the spirit."

Chapter 5

Summary

As a late moon rises outside, nearby motion rouses Kino from his sleep. In the pale light, he is barely able to discern Juana, who moves toward the fireplace, quietly gathers the pearl, and sneaks out into the night. Kino stealthily follows her as she heads toward the shore. When she hears him in pursuit, Juana breaks into a run, but Kino apprehends her just as she is preparing to hurl the pearl into the water. Grabbing the pearl from her, he punches her in the face and kicks her in the side when she falls down. As Kino hovers over Juana, the waves break upon her crumpled body. He hisses menacingly above her, then turns in disgust and leaves her without a word.

As Kino makes his way up the beach, a group of men assaults him. Kino struggles violently as they paw and prod at him. As Kino drives his knife into one of his attackers, the men knock the pearl from his grasp. Meanwhile, some distance away from the fight, Juana gets up on her knees and begins to make her way home. Climbing through the brush, she sees the pearl lying in the path. She picks it up and considers returning to the sea to discard the pearl once and for all.

At this moment, Juana spies two dark figures lying in the road and recognizes one of them as Kino. In the next instant, Juana realizes that Kino has killed the man slumped by his side. Juana drags the dead body into the brush and then helps Kino, who moans about losing his pearl. Juana silences him by showing him the pearl and explains that they must flee immediately because Kino has committed a horrible crime. Kino protests that he acted in self-defense, but Juana argues that his alibi won't matter at all to the authorities. Kino realizes that Juana is right, and they resolve to flee.

While Juana runs back to the brush house to grab Coyotito, Kino returns to the beach to ready his canoe for the escape. He finds that someone has punched a large hole in the boat's bottom. Filled with sorrow and rage, he quickly scrambles back to his brush house, moments before dawn. As he arrives in the vicinity of the neighborhood, he notices flames and realizes that his house is burning. As he runs toward the fire, Juana meets him with Coyotito in her arms. She confirms that their house has been burned down completely. As the neighbors rush to control the fire and to save their own houses, Kino, Juana, and Coyotito duck between the shadows and into Juan Tomás's house.

In the darkness inside Juan Tomás's house, Kino and Juana listen as the neighbors attempt to subdue the fire and speculate that Kino and Juana have been killed in the blaze. The couple can only listen as Juan Tomás's wife, Apolonia, wails in mourning for the loss of her relatives. When Apolonia returns to her house to change head shawls, Kino whispers to her, explaining that they are taking refuge. Kino instructs Apolonia to bring Juan Tomás to them and to keep their whereabouts a secret. She complies, and Juan Tomás arrives moments later, posting Apolonia at the door to keep watch while he talks with Kino.

Kino explains that he inadvertently killed a man after being attacked in the darkness. Juan Tomás blames this misfortune on the pearl and advises Kino to sell it without delay. Kino, however, is more focused on his losses, detailing the destruction of his canoe and his house. He implores Juan Tomás to hide them in his house for a night, until they can gather themselves and make a second attempt to flee. Juan Tomás hesitates to bring danger upon himself but ultimately agrees to shelter them and keep silent about their plans.

That afternoon, Kino and Juana crouch together in silence, listening to the neighbors discuss them among the ashes outside. Most of the neighbors assume that Kino and Juana are dead, but Juan Tomás suggests that perhaps the family has fled to the south to escape persecution. As he moves back and forth among the neighbors, he returns to his house from time to time, bringing bits and pieces of provisions that will help Kino and Juana on their journey.

That evening, Kino tells Juan Tomás his plan to travel to the cities of the north. Juan Tomás advises him to avoid the coast, as a search party will be on the lookout for him. When Juan Tomás asks if Kino still has the pearl, Kino responds that he does and that he intends to hold on to it. At dark, before the moon rises, Kino, Juana, and Coyotito exchange parting words with Juan Tomás and Apolonia, and head out into the night.

Analysis

Once Kino beats Juana, he begins to lose everything as rapidly as he gained the Pearl of the World. Kino loses his self-respect as a husband by beating Juana, his integrity as a law-abiding citizen by killing his attacker, his birthright in the form of the destroyed canoe, and his home, burned to the ground by an arsonist. Furthermore, Kino's senses become "dulled by his emotion" in his determination to overcome adversity and gain what he feels to be rightfully his by selling the pearl. He has lost the capacity to feel guilt, so he doesn't regret striking his wife or killing another man. As Kino's ambition to improve his family's lot strengthens, his ability to see to his family's well-being weakens. He exposes his son to questionable medical treatment and abuses his wife, all to achieve the material success he wants for them.

Kino's attempts to safeguard the pearl predispose him to violence in defense of his property. In the heat of battle, he loses control and succumbs to his basest human instincts: he murders his assailant. Once he crosses the line from defender to aggressor, Kino suddenly finds himself with nothing to gain and everything to lose. After Kino kills a man, the thought of *improving* his family is lost—the only thing that remains is to *save* himself and his family. Kino associates himself with his pearl, remarking to Juan Tomás that whereas he once might have given the pearl away as a gift, his many troubles have grafted the pearl to him. Kino sees the pearl as both a burden and a promise, and refuses to give it up.

Amid Kino's monomania (obsessive focus on a single idea), Juana remains tethered to and trapped in an increasingly disastrous situation. Though she sees Kino as "half insane and half god," she cannot imagine living without a man. Because of her position as a wife in a traditional society, Juana is necessarily subservient to Kino. She must follow what he views as his larger ambitions, even though her good sense cautions against it as their situation becomes increasingly desperate. Unfortunately, although Juana's good sense demands that the pearl—the essence of her former hopes—be thrown away, her subservience leads her to drag herself up and return the pearl to her husband.

Chapter 6

Summary

> *And once some large animal lumbered away, crackling the undergrowth as it went. And Kino gripped the handle of the big working knife and took a sense of protection from it.*
>
> *(See* QUOTATIONS, *p. 45)*

On a clear, windy night, Kino, Juana, and Coyotito begin their long march north, avoiding the sleeping town. Outside of town, they follow a road, carefully walking in a wheel rut to conceal their tracks. They walk all night and make camp in a roadside shelter at sunrise. After eating a small breakfast, Juana rests until midday. Kino spots a cluster of ants and lays down his foot as an obstacle. The ants climb over it, and he keeps his foot in place and watches them scale it.

When Juana rises, she asks Kino if he thinks they will be pursued. Juana then begins to doubt Kino's conviction that the pearl is worth far more than the dealers offered, but Kino points out that his attackers would not have tried to steal the pearl were it worth nothing. Kino stares at the pearl to read his future. He lies to Juana, telling her that he sees a rifle, a marriage in a church, and an education for Coyotito. In truth Kino sees a body bleeding on the ground,

Juana making her way home through the night after being beaten, and Coyotito's face swollen as though he were sick.

The family retreats farther into the shade for another rest. While Kino sleeps soundly, Juana is restless. As she plays with Coyotito, Kino wakes from a dream and demands that they keep quiet. Creeping forward, he spots a trio of trackers pursuing their trail. Kino stiffens and attempts to be still and silent until the trackers have passed. He watches them grow nearer and prepares to spring on them with his knife if necessary. Juana also hears the approaching trackers and does her best to quiet Coyotito.

The trackers' horse grows excited as the trackers approach the shelter. For a moment, it appears that they are poised to apprehend Coyotito and Juana, but eventually they lose their lead on the trail and move on. Kino realizes that it is only a matter of time before they return, and he runs quickly to Juana, telling her to gather up her things so that they can leave at once. Suddenly, Kino feels their cause to be hopeless and loses his will to flee, but Juana castigates him for giving up on his family. Finally, Kino suggests that they might be able to lose the trackers up in the mountains.

Kino and Juana collect their belongings and flee with Coyotito through the undergrowth, making no effort to conceal their tracks. As they climb the first rises, Kino realizes that the distance he is putting between his family and the trackers offers only a temporary fix to their problem. When Juana takes a rest with Coyotito, Kino proposes that she hide while he moves on ahead. Until the trackers have been diverted, she can take refuge in a nearby town. But, despite Kino's insistence, Juana refuses to split up, so the family moves on together.

As their ascent grows steeper, Kino attempts to vary and double back on their route to mislead the trackers. As the sun begins to set, Kino and Juana reach a nearby cleft and replenish their water supply at a pool and stream, where they drink to contentment, and Juana rinses Coyotito. From the lookout, Kino spies the trackers at a distance below, hurrying up the slope. Juana also realizes that they are still being pursued.

Kino deceives the trackers by creating a false trail up the cliff and descending again to take refuge with Juana and Coyotito in a nearby cave. Kino hopes that the trackers will climb past them, providing a chance for them to climb down the hill and out of range. Kino instructs Juana to keep Coyotito quiet, and they lie silently in the cave as twilight settles over the land.

By evening, the trackers arrive at the pool, where they make camp and eat. In the cave, Coyotito grows restless, and Juana quiets him. Kino notices that two of the men have settled in to sleep, while the third keeps watch. Kino realizes that if he can manage to stifle the lookout, he, Juana, and Coyotito will have a chance to escape. Juana fears for Kino's life, but Kino explains that they have no other choice. He instructs her to run to the nearest town should he be killed, and they part reluctantly.

Kino strips naked to avoid being seen by the watchman, and, after crouching at the cave entrance for a moment to survey his route, he springs forward. As Juana prays for him, Kino slowly moves down the slope toward the pool. Twenty feet from the trackers, he crouches behind a palm tree to ponder his next move. His muscles cramp and tremble, but he knows he must act quickly before the moon rises. He unsheathes his knife and prepares to attack. Just as he is poised to spring, the moon appears, and he realizes that his opportunity has been lost. Waiting for a moment when the watchman's head is turned, Kino gets ready to take a much riskier approach.

Suddenly, Coyotito lets out a cry that wakes one of the sleeping trackers. At first, they wonder if it could possibly be the cry of a human, or whether it is simply the cry of a coyote. The watchman decides to silence the wailer by shooting in the direction of the cry. Unbeknownst to Kino, the bullet hits and kills Coyotito. As the watchman shoots, Kino springs upon the trackers, stabbing the watchman and seizing the rifle. Knocking one of the other men out with a fierce blow, he watches as the last man attempts to flee up the cliff. The man makes little progress before Kino stops him with a first shot, and then murders him execution-style with another shot between the eyes. In the terrible moment that ensues, Kino notices the silence of the surrounding animals, and finally hears the blood-curdling cry issuing from his wife, mourning the death of Coyotito.

Later the next day, toward sunset, Kino and Juana walk side by side into La Paz, with Juana carrying Coyotito's corpse in a sack slung over her shoulder. They walk dazedly through the city, with unmoving eyes, speaking to no one. Onlookers stare wordlessly, and even Juan Tomás can only raise a hand in greeting.

Kino and Juana march through the town, past the brush houses, all the way to the sea. At the edge of the water, Kino stops and pulls the pearl from his pocket. Holding it up to the light, he stares into it carefully, and a flood of evil memories washes over him. Kino holds the pearl out in front of him, and then flings it out into the ocean. Kino and Juana watch the pearl as it splashes the surface, and stare at the spot quietly as the sun sets.

> Then the column [of ants] climbed over his instep and continued on its way, and Kino left his foot there and watched them move over it.
> (See QUOTATIONS, p. 42)

ANALYSIS

After their brush house is burned down and they are forced to flee their neighborhood, Kino and Juana find themselves in a struggle for survival in nature. Their state of nature ironically mimics that of the animals Kino observes contemplatively in Chapters 1 and 2. Exposed to the elements and the cries of coyotes, owls, and other animals, Kino thinks of himself as someone who has been taken over by some animal force. His peaceful, domestic life is a thing of the past.

As he does in Chapter 1, Kino here observes a cluster of ants. However, instead of watching "with the detachment of God" as he does before, Kino lays down his foot as an obstacle in the ants' path. The difference between these two acts symbolizes the way Kino's understanding of his relationship with nature has changed. Whereas earlier he is a detached observer, he now attempts to carve his own fate and rule in the natural world. But, as the ants reveal by easily finding their way around the obstacle Kino creates, Kino's attempts to rule over nature or twist it to his own devices have little effect, and nature has its way with him anyway.

While Kino does attempt to control the natural world, he also looks to it to guide his behavior when he gazes into the pearl "to find his vision" of the future. In the pearl, Kino sees his family's true fate, yet he mistakenly believes that denying what he sees and announcing an alternative vision will allow him to overcome his fate. Ultimately, Kino's base actions nullify the noble intentions he expresses in his speech. Kino announces to Juana that he envisions a grand wedding, but what the pearl reflects to him is the reality that he beats his wife. Kino also announces to Juana that he envisions an education for Coyotito, but in the pearl he sees the reality of "Coyotito's face, thick and feverish from the [doctor's] medicine."

Though she does not look into the pearl with Kino, Juana recognizes that Kino's visions are illusions grounded on ambition and hope. Her suggestion that the pearl has no real worth implicitly criticizes Kino's foolishness. Yet, when Kino considers giving up, Juana chastises him for his weakness. Her desire to continue suggests that her ambition is in fact just as fierce as Kino's. Like him, she allows her dreams for her family to lead her to ignore the reality of her situation and to attempt to overcome her fate. Her initial wish to secure a great pearl brings only grief to her family.

Steinbeck explicitly compares Kino and Juana to animals being chased by hunters. Like animals, the pair attempts to escape their pursuers by seeking out a higher elevation. What puts Kino and Juana in close proximity to the trackers is the need to be near water, a need common to all mammals. Furthermore, Kino finds himself forced to strip off his clothes, distinctive symbols of his humanity, in order to surprise his pursuers. In reverting to this animalistic strategy, Kino inadvertently transforms his own son into an animal, leading to Coyotito's death by an indiscriminate gunshot on the part of the trackers, who mistake the baby's cry for that of a coyote. Coyotito's name, which literally means "little coyote" in Spanish, foreshadows this transformation throughout the novella.

The narrator points out that in the animal world, water sources are both "places of life" and "places of death," because they offer a resource but also create competition between animals for the resource. This paradoxical status of the water pool parallels that of the pearl, which exerts both a positive and a destructive influence on Kino and Juana. Extrapolating further, the narrator's comment about the water source seems to apply to the entire material world—everyone both depends upon and competes for the material resources needed for survival.

Once the trackers are dead, Kino is free to continue to the city to sell his pearl, but Coyotito's death has stripped Kino of the motive for his struggle. Kino and Juana intended the pearl to facilitate the future they have dreamed of for their son, but the pearl's value is lost once Coyotito dies. The parable subtly evokes the story of Jesus, in that Kino, in attempting to play God by determining his own fate, sacrifices his son. Though an infant, Coyotito could be viewed as a martyr, since he dies for the sins of others. In this sense, Coyotito himself is the biblical "pearl of great price," the title Steinbeck originally planned to give his novella.

Critics are divided on the question of whether Kino's ultimate decision to rid himself of the pearl by throwing it back into the ocean represents a victory or a defeat. Some suggest that Kino's final act of material renunciation empowers him. The fact that the renunciation means that he will continue to live a life of poverty leads others to argue that Kino only adds to his tragedy in discarding the pearl. The narrator notes that as Kino and Juana reenter the town to dispose of the pearl, "the sun was behind them and their long shadows stalked ahead, and they seemed to carry two towers of darkness with them." This image symbolizes Kino and Juana's situation: their brightest days are behind them, and a dark patch of their own making lies ahead.

Important Quotations Explained

1. "In the town they tell the story of the great pearl—how it was found and how it was lost again. They tell of Kino, the fisherman, and of his wife, Juana, and of the baby, Coyotito. And because the story has been told so often, it has taken root in every man's mind. And, as with all retold tales that are in people's hearts, there are only good and bad things and black and white things and good and evil things and no in-between anywhere.

   "If this story is a parable, perhaps everyone takes his own meaning from it and reads his own life into it. In any case, they say in the town that. . . ."

This quotation is Steinbeck's epigraph to *The Pearl*. In introducing his novella as a legend (he first heard the legend of the Pearl of the World in a Mexican village), Steinbeck sets the tone for the story. He also establishes the parable's moral universe, in which there "are only good and bad things . . . and no in-between." Most important, the measured formal language of the epigraph evokes biblical verse and therefore suggests that *The Pearl* is a parable before Steinbeck himself even alludes to this possibility. Because the epigraph leads directly into Chapter 1 (the first sentence in Chapter 1 effectively concludes the unfinished final sentence of the epigraph), it also creates the sense that we have been taken directly to the source of the legend. The quotes that surround the epigraph give us the sense that someone is telling us a story and that the novella that follows is the storyteller's tale.

2. The ants were busy on the ground, big black ones with shiny bodies and the little dusty quick ants. Kino watched with the detachment of God while a dusty ant frantically tried to escape the sand trap an ant lion had dug for him.

   He watched the ants moving, a little column of them near to his foot, and he put his foot in their path. Then the column climbed over his instep and continued on its way, and Kino left his foot there and watched them move over it.

These two quotations are from Chapter 1 and Chapter 6, respectively. Kino's two encounters with ants are not important to the novel's plot, but they reveal a great deal about Kino's position and attitude at two key moments in the novel and thus form an important contrast with one another. The quotation from Chapter 1 occurs during the idyllic opening description of Kino and Juana's life. Kino's detached attitude toward nature suggests that he is a part of nature but also above it, like God. The description of the ant caught in the sand trap is a subtle instance of foreshadowing, as it mirrors Kino's eventual experience as a helpless prisoner of his own ambition.

The quotation from Chapter 6 describes Kino after the pearl has corrupted him. He is no longer detached from nature, and therefore he is no longer like God. Yet, as he becomes more animal-like, he aspires to be more like God by trying to affect the ants' behavior when he places his foot in their path. He does not succeed in changing nature, however; rather, nature simply renders him insignificant, as the ants methodically ignore him and climb over his shoe. As Kino's greed brings him from his initial human dignity to a plane closer to that of animals, he loses something essential to his humanity, as well as the easy, simple relationship with nature he enjoys early in the novella.

3. But the pearls were accidents, and the finding of one was luck, a little pat on the back by God or the gods or both.

This short quotation is from Chapter 2, when Kino prepares to make the dive on which he finds the Pearl of the World. The narrator contends that certain occurrences that shape human life are accidents willed by a divine power, events over which human beings have no control. It becomes clear that the discovery of pearls is a function of such seemingly arbitrary divine fate. Kino's eventual downfall can thus be seen as not entirely his own fault. The quotation also subtly alludes to the mixed cultural background of the natives in *The Pearl*: they come from a culture in which people believe in more than one god but have been governed for centuries by Catholic Spaniards who have built churches in which only a single God is worshipped. As a result, the natives are spiritually somewhat ambivalent, unsure as to whether the higher power in which they believe consists of "God" or "the gods."

4. In the pearl he saw Coyotito sitting at a little desk in a school, just as Kino had once seen it through an open door. And Coyotito was dressed in a jacket, and he had on a white collar and a broad silken tie. Moreover, Coyotito was writing on a big piece of paper. Kino looked at his neighbors fiercely. "My son will go to school," he said, and the neighbors were hushed. . . .

Kino's face shone with prophecy. "My son will read and open the books, and my son will write and will know writing. And my son will make numbers, and these things will make us free because he will know—he will know and through him we will know. . . . This is what the pearl will do."

This passage from Chapter 3 describes the moment of Kino's pivotal decision to direct all his energies toward using the pearl to obtain an education for Coyotito. Kino's ambition constitutes an attempt to shake the foundations of his society by placing his son on a level with the natives' European oppressors. The vehemence with which Kino reacts to his vision, as well as the hushed silence with which the neighbors hear it, is a testament to the improbable nature of Kino's plan not only to improve his son's lot but to break "free" of a centuries-long cycle of oppression. From this moment forward, Kino remains obsessed with his goal, which he can achieve only by making a great deal of money from his pearl. The image of Coyotito as an equal to the colonists transfixes Kino throughout the novella.

5. And the evils of the night were about them. The coyotes cried and laughed in the brush, and the owls screeched and hissed over their heads. And once some large animal lumbered away, crackling the undergrowth as it went. And Kino gripped the handle of the big working knife and took a sense of protection from it.

This quotation from Chapter 6 demonstrates how Kino's relationship with nature has changed, symbolizing his personal and moral downfall. In general, Steinbeck portrays the natural world positively in *The Pearl,* using beautiful language and images of sun-drenched scenery. This scene reverses that trend, as Steinbeck illustrates the dark and frightening aspect of nature. We sense that the universe itself opposes Kino's course of action. Kino himself reveals an adversarial relationship with nature by his defensive gripping of his knife handle to reassure himself. Where Kino earlier lived in harmony with nature, his ambition has made him nature's enemy.

Key Facts

FULL TITLE
The Pearl

AUTHOR
John Steinbeck

TYPE OF WORK
Novella

GENRE
Parable, allegory

LANGUAGE
English

TIME AND PLACE WRITTEN
1944–1945, California

DATE OF FIRST PUBLICATION
1945 (in serial form, where it was entitled "The Pearl of the World"), 1947 (in book form)

PUBLISHER
The Viking Press

NARRATOR
The anonymous narrator writes as if telling an old story he or she knows very well. The narrator frequently alludes to the story's ending and freely describes the inner thoughts and feelings of various characters. Rather than tell the story in his own voice, Steinbeck chooses to narrate in a stylized voice recalling that of a storyteller from a society like Kino's, in which stories are handed down from generation to generation, eventually losing their specificities and becoming moral parables, as Steinbeck insinuates in the opening epigraph, by virtue of sheer repetition.

POINT OF VIEW
The narrator uses third-person, omniscient narration, meaning he or she not only tells us what various characters think and feel but also provides analysis and commentary on the story.

The narrator shifts perspective frequently, focusing most often on Kino but occasionally focusing on other characters such as Juana and the doctor.

TONE

The narrator tells Kino's story to teach a moral lesson, and so treats Kino above all as a cautionary figure. At the same time, however, the narrator seems to see Kino as a sort of tragic hero, and is moved by the human weakness Kino's actions reveal. The narrator often shows a certain respect for Kino's striving to realize his ambitions—even while recognizing the mistakes Kino makes and mourning his ultimate moral downfall.

TENSE

Past

SETTING (TIME)

Unclear, possibly late nineteenth or early twentieth century

SETTING (PLACE)

A Mexican coastal village called La Paz, probably on the Baja Peninsula

PROTAGONIST

Kino

MAJOR CONFLICT

After finding a magnificent pearl, Kino seeks to sell it to acquire wealth. He wishes for his son's wound to heal, and for his son to obtain an education and become an equal to the European colonists who keep his people in a state of ignorance and poverty. When he tries to sell the pearl, however, Kino quickly meets resistance in the form of other people's greed. Ultimately, his struggle to acquire wealth places him at odds with his family, his culture, and nature, as Kino himself succumbs to greed and violence.

RISING ACTION

A scorpion stings Coyotito; Kino discovers a great pearl; Kino's attempts to sell the pearl are unsuccessful, and he is mysteriously attacked; Kino beats Juana for attempting to discard the pearl.

CLIMAX

Kino kills a man who attacks him for his pearl, an event that exposes the tension surrounding this object as a bringer of great evil as well as a chance for salvation.

FALLING ACTION

Kino and Juana flee the village and find themselves chased by trackers; Kino fights with the trackers, not knowing that they have taken Coyotito's cry to be that of a coyote and shot him; Kino and Juana return to the village and throw the pearl back into the sea.

THEMES

Greed as a destructive force; the roles of fate and agency in shaping human life; colonial society's oppression of native cultures

MOTIFS

Nature imagery, Kino's songs

SYMBOLS

The pearl, the scorpion, Kino's canoe

FORESHADOWING

Coyotito's name; the discussion of "The Pearl That Might Be"; Juana's prayer for Kino to find a great pearl; Juana and Juan Tomás's warnings to Kino that the pearl is dangerous

Study Questions

1. *What do we learn about the pearl's symbolism from the reactions it evokes?*

In his epigraph to *The Pearl*, Steinbeck writes, "If this story is a parable, perhaps everyone takes his own meaning from it and reads his own life into it." Indeed, the pearl's vague symbolism means that each character's—and each reader's—reaction to it seems more a function of the nature of the person involved than of the pearl itself. For most characters, the pearl simply brings out greed and ambition. To those few who are sensitive to the current of greed surrounding the pearl, however, the pearl is a powerful symbol of evil and ill fortune. Juana is one such character, as is Juan Tomás, who quickly recognizes the "devil in th[e] pearl."

2. *Discuss Steinbeck's use of foreshadowing in* The Pearl.

At every turn, Steinbeck provides clues as to what will happen in the narrative, although sometimes his clues are obscure. For instance, Coyotito's name, which means "little coyote," hints at the fact that Coyotito is eventually mistaken for a baby coyote by the trackers. More concretely, in Chapter 2 the narrator discusses the native's concept of "the Pearl That Might Be," foreshadowing Kino's discovery of "the Pearl of the World." Additionally, Juana suggests that the pearl is evil long before it has visited its full measure of evil upon them. Near the end of Chapter 3, Juana even suggests that the pearl will destroy their son, as it ultimately does.

3. *One important element of* The Pearl *is the contrast between fate and human agency, between the destiny that is made for us and the destiny that we make ourselves. How do these forces interact in Kino's story? To what extent is Kino responsible for his own demise? To what extent is fate responsible?*

The role of fate looms large in Kino's undoing in two ways. First, Kino's downfall is incited by his accidental, divinely appointed discovery of the pearl. Second, Kino's status as an impoverished fisherman who lives under the burden of colonial oppression also creates the sense that his tragedy is decreed by fate. The odds weigh heavily against his success, and it must be granted that, to some extent, society does conspire toward his downfall.

At the same time, Kino is in large part to blame for his misfortunes. His headstrong insistence on profit at all cost and his refusal to heed the warnings of his brother and his wife demonstrate his stubbornness and heedlessness; his excessive dependence on violence betrays a possible recklessness and poor judgment. Ultimately, Kino's own shortcomings are the cause of the destruction of his happy family life.

How to Write Literary Analysis

The Literary Essay: A Step-by-Step Guide

When you read for pleasure, your only goal is enjoyment. You might find yourself reading to get caught up in an exciting story, to learn about an interesting time or place, or just to pass time. Maybe you're looking for inspiration, guidance, or a reflection of your own life. There are as many different, valid ways of reading a book as there are books in the world.

When you read a work of literature in an English class, however, you're being asked to read in a special way: you're being asked to perform *literary analysis*. To analyze something means to break it down into smaller parts and then examine how those parts work, both individually and together. Literary analysis involves examining all the parts of a novel, play, short story, or poem—elements such as character, setting, tone, and imagery—and thinking about how the author uses those elements to create certain effects.

A literary essay isn't a book review: you're not being asked whether or not you liked a book or whether you'd recommend it to another reader. A literary essay also isn't like the kind of book report you wrote when you were younger, where your teacher wanted you to summarize the book's action. A high school- or college-level literary essay asks, "How does this piece of literature actually work?" "How does it do what it does?" and, "Why might the author have made the choices he or she did?"

The Seven Steps
No one is born knowing how to analyze literature; it's a skill you learn and a process you can master. As you gain more practice with this kind of thinking and writing, you'll be able to craft a method that works best for you. But until then, here are seven basic steps to writing a well-constructed literary essay:

1. Ask questions
2. Collect evidence
3. Construct a thesis

4. *Develop and organize arguments*
5. *Write the introduction*
6. *Write the body paragraphs*
7. *Write the conclusion*

1. Ask Questions

When you're assigned a literary essay in class, your teacher will often provide you with a list of writing prompts. Lucky you! Now all you have to do is choose one. Do yourself a favor and pick a topic that interests you. You'll have a much better (not to mention easier) time if you start off with something you enjoy thinking about. If you are asked to come up with a topic by yourself, though, you might start to feel a little panicked. Maybe you have too many ideas—or none at all. Don't worry. Take a deep breath and start by asking yourself these questions:

- **What struck you?** Did a particular image, line, or scene linger in your mind for a long time? If it fascinated you, chances are you can draw on it to write a fascinating essay.

- **What confused you?** Maybe you were surprised to see a character act in a certain way, or maybe you didn't understand why the book ended the way it did. Confusing moments in a work of literature are like a loose thread in a sweater: if you pull on it, you can unravel the entire thing. Ask yourself why the author chose to write about that character or scene the way he or she did and you might tap into some important insights about the work as a whole.

- **Did you notice any patterns?** Is there a phrase that the main character uses constantly or an image that repeats throughout the book? If you can figure out how that pattern weaves through the work and what the significance of that pattern is, you've almost got your entire essay mapped out.

- **Did you notice any contradictions or ironies?** Great works of literature are complex; great literary essays recognize and explain those complexities. Maybe the title (*Happy Days*) totally disagrees with the book's subject matter (hungry orphans dying in the woods). Maybe the main character acts one way around his family and a completely different way around his friends and associates. If you can find a way to explain a work's contradictory elements, you've got the seeds of a great essay.

At this point, you don't need to know exactly what you're going to say about your topic; you just need a place to begin your exploration. You can help direct your reading and brainstorming by formulating your topic as a *question,* which you'll then try to answer in your essay. The best questions invite critical debates and discussions, not just a rehashing of the summary. Remember, you're looking for something you can *prove or argue* based on evidence you find in the text. Finally, remember to keep the scope of your question in mind: is this a topic you can adequately address within the word or page limit you've been given? Conversely, is this a topic big enough to fill the required length?

GOOD QUESTIONS
> *"Are Romeo and Juliet's parents responsible for the deaths of their children?"*
> *"Why do pigs keep showing up in* LORD OF THE FLIES*?"*
> *"Are Dr. Frankenstein and his monster alike? How?"*

BAD QUESTIONS
> *"What happens to Scout in* TO KILL A MOCKINGBIRD*?"*
> *"What do the other characters in* JULIUS CAESAR *think about Caesar?"*
> *"How does Hester Prynne in* THE SCARLET LETTER *remind me of my sister?"*

---

2. COLLECT EVIDENCE

Once you know what question you want to answer, it's time to scour the book for things that will help you answer the question. Don't worry if you don't know what you want to say yet—right now you're just collecting ideas and material and letting it all percolate. Keep track of passages, symbols, images, or scenes that deal with your topic. Eventually, you'll start making connections between these examples and your thesis will emerge.

Here's a brief summary of the various parts that compose each and every work of literature. These are the elements that you will analyze in your essay, and which you will offer as evidence to support your arguments. For more on the parts of literary works, see the Glossary of Literary Terms at the end of this section.

ELEMENTS OF STORY   These are the *what*s of the work—what happens, where it happens, and to whom it happens.

- **Plot:** All of the events and actions of the work.
- **Character:** The people who act and are acted upon in a literary work. The main character of a work is known as the *protagonist*.
- **Conflict:** The central tension in the work. In most cases, the protagonist wants something, while opposing forces (antagonists) hinder the protagonist's progress.
- **Setting:** When and where the work takes place. Elements of setting include location, time period, time of day, weather, social atmosphere, and economic conditions.
- **Narrator:** The person telling the story. The narrator may straightforwardly report what happens, convey the subjective opinions and perceptions of one or more characters, or provide commentary and opinion in his or her own voice.
- **Themes:** The main idea or message of the work—usually an abstract idea about people, society, or life in general. A work may have many themes, which may be in tension with one another.

ELEMENTS OF STYLE   These are the *how*s—how the characters speak, how the story is constructed, and how language is used throughout the work.

- **Structure and organization:** How the parts of the work are assembled. Some novels are narrated in a linear, chronological fashion, while others skip around in time. Some plays follow a traditional three- or five-act structure, while others are a series of loosely connected scenes. Some authors deliberately leave gaps in their works, leaving readers to puzzle out the missing information. A work's structure and organization can tell you a lot about the kind of message it wants to convey.
- **Point of view:** The perspective from which a story is told. In *first-person point of view*, the narrator involves him or herself in the story. ("I went to the store"; "We watched in horror as the bird slammed into the window.") A first-person narrator is usually the protagonist of the work, but not always. In *third-person point of view*, the narrator does not participate

in the story. A third-person narrator may closely follow a specific character, recounting that individual character's thoughts or experiences, or it may be what we call an *omniscient* narrator. Omniscient narrators see and know all: they can witness any event in any time or place and are privy to the inner thoughts and feelings of all characters. Remember that the narrator and the author are not the same thing!

- **Diction:** Word choice. Whether a character uses dry, clinical language or flowery prose with lots of exclamation points can tell you a lot about his or her attitude and personality.
- **Syntax:** Word order and sentence construction. Syntax is a crucial part of establishing an author's narrative voice. Ernest Hemingway, for example, is known for writing in very short, straightforward sentences, while James Joyce characteristically wrote in long, incredibly complicated lines.
- **Tone:** The mood or feeling of the text. Diction and syntax often contribute to the tone of a work. A novel written in short, clipped sentences that use small, simple words might feel brusque, cold, or matter-of-fact.
- **Imagery:** Language that appeals to the senses, representing things that can be seen, smelled, heard, tasted, or touched.
- **Figurative language:** Language that is not meant to be interpreted literally. The most common types of figurative language are *metaphors* and *similes,* which compare two unlike things in order to suggest a similarity between them—for example, "All the world's a stage," or "The moon is like a ball of green cheese." (Metaphors say one thing *is* another thing; similes claim that one thing is *like* another thing.)

3. Construct a Thesis

When you've examined all the evidence you've collected and know how you want to answer the question, it's time to write your thesis statement. A *thesis* is a claim about a work of literature that needs to be supported by evidence and arguments. The thesis statement is the heart of the literary essay, and the bulk of your paper will be spent trying to prove this claim. A good thesis will be:

- **Arguable.** "*The Great Gatsby* describes New York society in the 1920s" isn't a thesis—it's a fact.

- **Provable through textual evidence**. "*Hamlet* is a confusing but ultimately very well-written play" is a weak thesis because it offers the writer's personal opinion about the book. Yes, it's arguable, but it's not a claim that can be proved or supported with examples taken from the play itself.
- **Surprising**. "Both George and Lenny change a great deal in *Of Mice and Men*" is a weak thesis because it's obvious. A really strong thesis will argue for a reading of the text that is not immediately apparent.
- **Specific**. "Dr. Frankenstein's monster tells us a lot about the human condition" is *almost* a really great thesis statement, but it's still too vague. What does the writer mean by "a lot"? *How* does the monster tell us so much about the human condition?

Good Thesis Statements

Question: In *Romeo and Juliet*, which is more powerful in shaping the lovers' story: fate or foolishness?

Thesis: "Though Shakespeare defines Romeo and Juliet as 'star-crossed lovers' and images of stars and planets appear throughout the play, a closer examination of that celestial imagery reveals that the stars are merely witnesses to the characters' foolish activities and not the causes themselves."

Question: How does the bell jar function as a symbol in Sylvia Plath's *The Bell Jar*?

Thesis: "A bell jar is a bell-shaped glass that has three basic uses: to hold a specimen for observation, to contain gases, and to maintain a vacuum. The bell jar appears in each of these capacities in *The Bell Jar*, Plath's semi-autobiographical novel, and each appearance marks a different stage in Esther's mental breakdown."

Question: Would Piggy in *The Lord of the Flies* make a good island leader if he were given the chance?

Thesis: "Though the intelligent, rational, and innovative Piggy has the mental characteristics of a good leader, he ultimately lacks the social skills necessary to be an effective one. Golding emphasizes this point by giving Piggy a foil in the charismatic Jack, whose magnetic personality allows him to capture and wield power effectively, if not always wisely."

4. Develop and Organize Arguments

The reasons and examples that support your thesis will form the middle paragraphs of your essay. Since you can't really write your thesis statement until you know how you'll structure your argument, you'll probably end up working on steps 3 and 4 at the same time.

There's no single method of argumentation that will work in every context. One essay prompt might ask you to compare and contrast two characters, while another asks you to trace an image through a given work of literature. These questions require different kinds of answers and therefore different kinds of arguments. Below, we'll discuss three common kinds of essay prompts and some strategies for constructing a solid, well-argued case.

Types of Literary Essays

- **Compare and contrast**

    Compare and contrast the characters of Huck and Jim in The Adventures of Huckleberry Finn.

    Chances are you've written this kind of essay before. In an academic literary context, you'll organize your arguments the same way you would in any other class. You can either go *subject by subject* or *point by point*. In the former, you'll discuss one character first and then the second. In the latter, you'll choose several traits (attitude toward life, social status, images and metaphors associated with the character) and devote a paragraph to each. You may want to use a mix of these two approaches—for example, you may want to spend a paragraph apiece broadly sketching Huck's and Jim's personalities before transitioning into a paragraph or two that describes a few key points of comparison. This can be a highly effective strategy if you want to make a counterintuitive argument—that, despite seeming to be totally different, the two objects being compared are actually similar in a very important way (or vice versa). Remember that your essay should reveal something fresh or unexpected about the text, so think beyond the obvious parallels and differences.

- **Trace**

    Choose an image—for example, birds, knives, or eyes—and trace that image throughout Macbeth.

    Sounds pretty easy, right? All you need to do is read the play, underline every appearance of a knife in *Macbeth,* and then list them in your essay in the order they appear, right? Well, not exactly. Your teacher doesn't want a simple catalog of examples. He or she wants to see you make *connections* between those examples—that's the difference between summarizing and analyzing. In the *Macbeth* example above, think about the different contexts in which knives appear in the play and to what effect. In *Macbeth*, there are real knives and imagined knives; knives that kill and knives that simply threaten. Categorize and classify your examples to give them some order. Finally, always keep the overall effect in mind. After you choose and analyze your examples, you should come to some greater understanding about the work, as well as your chosen image, symbol, or phrase's role in developing the major themes and stylistic strategies of that work.

- **Debate**

    Is the society depicted in 1984 good for its citizens?

    In this kind of essay, you're being asked to debate a moral, ethical, or aesthetic issue regarding the work. You might be asked to judge a character or group of characters (*Is Caesar responsible for his own demise?*) or the work itself (*Is JANE EYRE a feminist novel?*). For this kind of essay, there are two important points to keep in mind. First, don't simply base your arguments on your personal feelings and reactions. Every literary essay expects you to read and analyze the work, so search for evidence in the text. What do characters in *1984* have to say about the government of Oceania? What images does Orwell use that might give you a hint about his attitude toward the government? As in any debate, you also need to make sure that you define all the necessary terms before you begin to argue your case. What does it mean to be a "good" society? What makes a novel "feminist"? You should define your terms right up front, in the first paragraph after your introduction.

    Second, remember that strong literary essays make contrary and surprising arguments. Try to think outside the box. In the *1984* example above, it seems like the obvious answer would be no, the totalitarian society depicted in Orwell's novel is *not* good for its citizens. But can you think of any arguments for the opposite side? Even if your final assertion is that the novel depicts a cruel, repressive, and therefore harmful society, acknowledging and responding to the counterargument will strengthen your overall case.

5. Write the Introduction

Your introduction sets up the entire essay. It's where you present your topic and articulate the particular issues and questions you'll be addressing. It's also where you, as the writer, introduce yourself to your readers. A persuasive literary essay immediately establishes its writer as a knowledgeable, authoritative figure.

An introduction can vary in length depending on the overall length of the essay, but in a traditional five-paragraph essay it should be no longer than one paragraph. However long it is, your introduction needs to:

- **Provide any necessary context.** Your introduction should situate the reader and let him or her know what to expect. What book are you discussing? Which characters? What topic will you be addressing?
- **Answer the "So what?" question.** Why is this topic important, and why is your particular position on the topic noteworthy? Ideally, your introduction should pique the reader's interest by suggesting how your argument is surprising or otherwise counterintuitive. Literary essays make unexpected connections and reveal less-than-obvious truths.
- **Present your thesis.** This usually happens at or very near the end of your introduction.
- **Indicate the shape of the essay to come.** Your reader should finish reading your introduction with a good sense of the scope of your essay as well as the path you'll take toward proving your thesis. You don't need to spell out every step, but you do need to suggest the organizational pattern you'll be using.

Your introduction should not:

- **Be vague.** Beware of the two killer words in literary analysis: *interesting* and *important*. Of course the work, question, or example is interesting and important—that's why you're writing about it!
- **Open with any grandiose assertions.** Many student readers think that beginning their essays with a flamboyant statement such as, "Since the dawn of time, writers have been fascinated with the topic of free will," makes them

sound important and commanding. You know what? It actually sounds pretty amateurish.

- **Wildly praise the work.** Another typical mistake student writers make is extolling the work or author. Your teacher doesn't need to be told that "Shakespeare is perhaps the greatest writer in the English language." You can mention a work's reputation in passing—by referring to *The Adventures of Huckleberry Finn* as "Mark Twain's enduring classic," for example—but don't make a point of bringing it up unless that reputation is key to your argument.

- **Go off-topic.** Keep your introduction streamlined and to the point. Don't feel the need to throw in all kinds of bells and whistles in order to impress your reader—just get to the point as quickly as you can, without skimping on any of the required steps.

6. Write the Body Paragraphs

Once you've written your introduction, you'll take the arguments you developed in step 4 and turn them into your body paragraphs. The organization of this middle section of your essay will largely be determined by the argumentative strategy you use, but no matter how you arrange your thoughts, your body paragraphs need to do the following:

- **Begin with a strong topic sentence.** Topic sentences are like signs on a highway: they tell the reader where they are and where they're going. A good topic sentence not only alerts readers to what issue will be discussed in the following paragraph but also gives them a sense of what argument will be made *about* that issue. "Rumor and gossip play an important role in *The Crucible*" isn't a strong topic sentence because it doesn't tell us very much. "The community's constant gossiping creates an environment that allows false accusations to flourish" is a much stronger topic sentence—it not only tells us *what* the paragraph will discuss (gossip) but *how* the paragraph will discuss the topic (by showing how gossip creates a set of conditions that leads to the play's climactic action).

- **Fully and completely develop a single thought.** Don't skip around in your paragraph or try to stuff in too much material. Body paragraphs are like bricks: each individual one needs to be strong and sturdy or the entire structure will collapse. Make sure you have really proven your point before moving on to the next one.

- **Use transitions effectively.** Good literary essay writers know that each paragraph must be clearly and strongly linked to the material around it. Think of each paragraph as a response to the one that precedes it. Use transition words and phrases such as *however, similarly, on the contrary, therefore,* and *furthermore* to indicate what kind of response you're making.

7. Write the Conclusion

Just as you used the introduction to ground your readers in the topic before providing your thesis, you'll use the conclusion to quickly summarize the specifics learned thus far and then hint at the broader implications of your topic. A good conclusion will:

- **Do more than simply restate the thesis.** If your thesis argued that *The Catcher in the Rye* can be read as a Christian allegory, don't simply end your essay by saying, "And that is why *The Catcher in the Rye* can be read as a Christian allegory." If you've constructed your arguments well, this kind of statement will just be redundant.

- **Synthesize the arguments, not summarize them.** Similarly, don't repeat the details of your body paragraphs in your conclusion. The reader has already read your essay, and chances are it's not so long that they've forgotten all your points by now.

- **Revisit the "So what?" question.** In your introduction, you made a case for why your topic and position are important. You should close your essay with the same sort of gesture. What do your readers know now that they didn't know before? How will that knowledge help them better appreciate or understand the work overall?

- **Move from the specific to the general.** Your essay has most likely treated a very specific element of the work—a single character, a small set of images, or a particular passage. In your conclusion, try to show how this narrow discussion has wider implications for the work overall. If your essay on *To Kill a Mockingbird* focused on the character of Boo Radley, for example, you might want to include a bit in your conclusion about how he fits into the novel's larger message about childhood, innocence, or family life.

- **Stay relevant.** Your conclusion should suggest new directions of thought, but it shouldn't be treated as an opportunity to pad your essay with all the extra, interesting ideas you came up with during your brainstorming sessions but couldn't fit into the essay proper. Don't attempt to stuff in unrelated queries or too many abstract thoughts.

- **Avoid making overblown closing statements.** A conclusion should open up your highly specific, focused discussion, but it should do so without drawing a sweeping lesson about life or human nature. Making such observations may be part of the point of reading, but it's almost always a mistake in essays, where these observations tend to sound overly dramatic or simply silly.

A+ Essay Checklist

Congratulations! If you've followed all the steps we've outlined above, you should have a solid literary essay to show for all your efforts. What if you've got your sights set on an A+? To write the kind of superlative essay that will be rewarded with a perfect grade, keep the following rubric in mind. These are the qualities that teachers expect to see in a truly A+ essay. How does yours stack up?

- ✓ Demonstrates a thorough understanding of the book
- ✓ Presents an original, compelling argument
- ✓ Thoughtfully analyzes the text's formal elements
- ✓ Uses appropriate and insightful examples
- ✓ Structures ideas in a logical and progressive order
- ✓ Demonstrates a mastery of sentence construction, transitions, grammar, spelling, and word choice

Suggested Essay Topics

1. How does the novella's conclusion complete Steinbeck's moral argument? Could the novella have ended in any other way? Is it wise of Kino to throw the pearl back into the sea, or should he have searched for another option?

2. What role does family play in THE PEARL? How does the loyalty of Kino's family members (especially Juana and Juan Tomás) affect his actions? Was Juan Tomás correct to shield Kino from the law after he had committed murder? Is Juana correct to be so submissive to him? Does either character have a choice?

3. Some critics read THE PEARL as a very specific critique of the American dream of wealth and success. Is this reading plausible, or does it limit it unnecessarily? If the story is about the American dream, why is it set in a colonial Mexican society?

A+ Student Essay

> A parable is a brief, didactic story with flat characters, passed down orally from generation to generation. To what extent is *The Pearl* a parable?

On the surface, *The Pearl* resembles a novella. Its length, its attention to a protagonist's inner life, and its occasional moments of lyricism are hallmarks of that literary form. On the other hand, Steinbeck's style is often conversational and bland, as if he were speaking the story instead of writing it. His characters have little depth, each showing a remarkably consistent pattern of good or evil actions, each illustrating Steinbeck's idea that wealth is a force of corruption. By grafting the conventions of a parable onto the structure of a novella, Steinbeck creates an awkward hybrid that lacks the finer qualities of either genre.

The Pearl has some superficial aspects of a novella. Its length—eighty-seven pages—and its division into short chapters suggest that it is a novel in miniature, a piece of prose that concisely portrays one character's soul. Its moments of interior description, the sounds of "The Song of the Enemy" and "The Song of the Family" beating in Kino's ears, lead us to believe that Steinbeck is interested in Kino's psychology. The lyrical scene-setting passages—the "shimmering scarves" of the hot yellow sun—have the rich, literary quality of a novella, instead of the plainness of a parable. For these reasons, it's tempting to classify *The Pearl* alongside Steinbeck's own classic novella *Of Mice and Men*, a slim volume that probes the inner life of the impoverished worker George.

Yet large portions of Steinbeck's writing are colorless and monotonous, as if he were recalling the story around a campfire. Again and again, sentences begin with "And"—an incantatory device that appears frequently in English translations of Biblical parables. There are four "And" sentences on page sixty-seven; five on sixty-four. Steinbeck also repeatedly strings together independent clauses with "and": "Kino held the great pearl in his hand, and it was warm and alive . . ." "Kino looked into his pearl, and Juana cast her eyelashes down . . ." Steinbeck eschews the syntactical variety—gerunds, colons, long sentences interspersed with short—that we would expect from a literary artist. The flatness of his style recalls the plain, repetitive language of a parable.

More striking is the shallowness of Steinbeck's characterizations. Frequently, when he writes about the evil doctor, the doctor is sitting in bed dribbling chocolate on his sheets. The doctor's interactions with Kino—denying him help, then offering it when he suspects he can make money—are predictably immoral; Steinbeck does not attempt to humanize him or explain why he acts in such a consistently cruel way. The pearl buyers are interchangeable; each beady-eyed buyer denies Kino a fair deal, and Steinbeck does not make clear distinctions among their personalities. Even Kino, the protagonist, lacks a convincing inner life. Steinbeck's shorthand for Kino's feelings toward Juana and Coyotito—the mysterious strains of "The Song of the Family"—makes us wonder what is happening in Kino's head, what he thinks about his wife, and how his ever-shifting thoughts affect the smallest details of his domestic interactions. Steinbeck uses the doctor, the money-lender, and Kino to show the demoralizing influence of wealth on all mankind. Like a writer of a parable, Steinbeck does not try to convince us that these characters are human beings.

By blending conventions of the novella and the parable, Steinbeck writes a ninety-page lecture on the evils of material wealth. The length and lyrical descriptions lead us to anticipate a novella, complete with the subtlety and psychological insight associated with that genre. On the other hand, the simple characters and oral quality of the writing lead us to anticipate a parable, with the force and concision associated with that genre. *The Pearl*'s awkward combination of literary styles may account for its poor reception among many critics, who have argued that Steinbeck stopped writing well after *The Grapes of Wrath*.

Glossary of Literary Terms

ANTAGONIST
The entity that acts to frustrate the goals of the *protagonist*. The antagonist is usually another *character* but may also be a non-human force.

ANTIHERO / ANTIHEROINE
A *protagonist* who is not admirable or who challenges notions of what should be considered admirable.

CHARACTER
A person, animal, or any other thing with a personality that appears in a *narrative*.

CLIMAX
The moment of greatest intensity in a text or the major turning point in the *plot*.

CONFLICT
The central struggle that moves the *plot* forward. The conflict can be the *protagonist*'s struggle against fate, nature, society, or another person.

FIRST-PERSON POINT OF VIEW
A literary style in which the *narrator* tells the story from his or her own *point of view* and refers to himself or herself as "I." The narrator may be an active participant in the story or just an observer.

HERO / HEROINE
The principal *character* in a literary work or *narrative*.

IMAGERY
Language that brings to mind sense-impressions, representing things that can be seen, smelled, heard, tasted, or touched.

MOTIF
A recurring idea, structure, contrast, or device that develops or informs the major *themes* of a work of literature.

NARRATIVE
A story.

NARRATOR
   The person (sometimes a *character*) who tells a story; the *voice* assumed by the writer. The narrator and the author of the work of literature are not the same person.

PLOT
   The arrangement of the events in a story, including the sequence in which they are told, the relative emphasis they are given, and the causal connections between events.

POINT OF VIEW
   The *perspective* that a *narrative* takes toward the events it describes.

PROTAGONIST
   The main *character* around whom the story revolves.

SETTING
   The location of a *narrative* in time and space. Setting creates mood or atmosphere.

SUBPLOT
   A secondary *plot* that is of less importance to the overall story but may serve as a point of contrast or comparison to the main plot.

SYMBOL
   An object, *character,* figure, or color that is used to represent an abstract idea or concept. Unlike an *emblem,* a symbol may have different meanings in different contexts.

SYNTAX
   The way the words in a piece of writing are put together to form lines, phrases, or clauses; the basic structure of a piece of writing.

THEME
   A fundamental and universal idea explored in a literary work.

TONE
   The author's attitude toward the subject or *characters* of a story or poem or toward the reader.

VOICE
   An author's individual way of using language to reflect his or her own personality and attitudes. An author communicates voice through *tone, diction,* and *syntax.*

A Note on Plagiarism

Plagiarism—presenting someone else's work as your own—rears its ugly head in many forms. Many students know that copying text without citing it is unacceptable. But some don't realize that even if you're not quoting directly, but instead are paraphrasing or summarizing, *it is plagiarism* unless you cite the source.

Here are the most common forms of plagiarism:

- Using an author's phrases, sentences, or paragraphs without citing the source
- Paraphrasing an author's ideas without citing the source
- Passing off another student's work as your own

How do you steer clear of plagiarism? You should *always* acknowledge all words and ideas that aren't your own by using quotation marks around verbatim text or citations like footnotes and endnotes to note another writer's ideas. For more information on how to give credit when credit is due, ask your teacher for guidance or visit www.sparknotes.com.

Review & Resources

Quiz

1. Where is *The Pearl* set?

    A. Spain
    B. Mexico
    C. Cuba
    D. The United States

2. What stings Coyotito?

    A. A porcupine
    B. A hornet
    C. A scorpion
    D. A mosquito

3. With what does Kino offer to pay the doctor?

    A. Eight small pearls
    B. Five pieces of gold bullion
    C. Ten weeks of hard labor
    D. His canoe

4. How does Kino react when the doctor snubs him?

    A. He sulks
    B. He strikes the front gate with his fists, bloodying his knuckles
    C. He phones his lawyer
    D. He threatens the doctor with death

5. What does Juana use as a poultice for Coyotito's wound?

    A. Dry ice
    B. Peppermint
    C. Oatmeal
    D. Seaweed

6. How did Kino acquire his canoe?

   A. He built it
   B. He exchanged pearls for it
   C. He inherited it
   D. He stole it

7. For what does Juana pray when she is in the canoe?

   A. A big pearl
   B. Rain
   C. Coyotito's health
   D. Sinners

8. Which of the following is not on the list of things Kino plans to buy with his newfound wealth?

   A. An education for Coyotito
   B. A sailboat
   C. A rifle
   D. A proper marriage in a church

9. How does the doctor treat Coyotito's scorpion wound?

   A. With a capsule filled with powder
   B. With a strange purple liquid
   C. By administering a shot
   D. By wrapping it in seaweed

10. Where does Kino hide the pearl during the night?

    A. In the doctor's safe
    B. In his sock
    C. Under the potted plant by the toolbox
    D. Beneath his sleeping mat

11. What is the name of the town where Kino first attempts to sell his pearl?

    A. Santa Lucia
    B. La Paz
    C. Cadaques
    D. Tegucigalpa

THE PEARL 73

12. What is the first pearl dealer's nervous habit?

    A. He manipulates a coin in his hands
    B. He twiddles his thumbs
    C. He taps his foot
    D. He chain-smokes

13. What is the best offer Kino gets for his pearl?

    A. 5,000 pesetas
    B. 1,000 pesos
    C. 1,500 pesos
    D. 20 pounds sterling

14. What reason does the dealer give for not liking Kino's pearl?

    A. It is too large
    B. It smells funny
    C. It is actually made out of beeswax
    D. It is stolen

15. How does Kino decide to make money when he realizes that the local pearl dealers are lowballing him?

    A. By panhandling and singing for money
    B. By stockpiling all the pearls of La Paz
    C. By traveling to the capital to sell his pearl
    D. By filing a lawsuit against the dealers according to the Sherman Anti-Trust Act of 1890

16. What does Juana propose to do with the pearl?

    A. Have it set in a silver necklace that she can wear on formal occasions
    B. Throw it back into the sea
    C. Give it to Coyotito
    D. Sell it to the highest bidder as soon as possible

17. How does Kino react when Juana attempts to steal the pearl from him?

    A. He agrees with her that the pearl will only bring them evil
    B. He punches her in the head and then kicks her
    C. He leaves her for another woman
    D. He chases her down and persuades her to return the pearl to him

18. Why must Kino and his family flee from their neighborhood?

    A. Because Kino sets fire to a group of houses
    B. Because Kino steals a knife from his brother
    C. Because Kino makes advances on his brother's wife
    D. Because Kino kills a man

19. Where do Kino and Juana first take refuge after their house burns down?

    A. In a cave by the beach
    B. In their canoe
    C. At Juan Tomás's house
    D. In the forest

20. Where do Kino and Juana flee to escape the trackers?

    A. Down the river
    B. Up the mountain
    C. Through the vale
    D. To their underwater lair

21. What does Kino do to conceal himself from the trackers?

    A. He dons camouflage
    B. He strips naked
    C. He cuts his hair
    D. He grows a moustache

22. For what do the trackers mistake Coyotito's cry?

    A. A coyote's cry
    B. An owl's screech
    C. A cat's meow
    D. A bat's shriek

23. How does Kino rid himself of the trackers?

    A. He wrestles them into submission
    B. He outruns them
    C. He hides until they have lost his trail
    D. He kills them

24. How does Coyotito die?

    A. He falls off a cliff
    B. He is shot
    C. A scorpion poisons him
    D. He starves

25. What does Kino do with the pearl at the novella's end?

    A. He donates it to charity
    B. He sells it to the highest bidder
    C. He buries it in his brother's house
    D. He throws it back into the sea

ANSWER KEY

1: B; 2: C; 3: A; 4: B; 5: D; 6: C; 7: A; 8: B; 9: A; 10: D; 11: B; 12: A; 13: C; 14: A; 15: C; 16: B; 17: B; 18: D; 19: C; 20: B; 21: B; 22: A; 23: D; 24: B; 25: D

Suggestions for Further Reading

BENSON, JACKSON J., ed. *The Short Novels of John Steinbeck: Critical Essays with a Checklist to Steinbeck Criticism.* Durham, North Carolina: Duke University Press, 1990.

BURKHEAD, CYNTHIA. *Student Companion to John Steinbeck.* Westport: Greenwood Press, 2002.

GRAY, JAMES. *John Steinbeck.* Minneapolis: University of Minnesota Press, 1971.

JOHNSON, CLAUDIA DURST. *Understanding* OF MICE AND MEN, THE RED PONY, *and* THE PEARL: *A Student Casebook to Issues, Sources, and Historical Documents.* Westport: Greenwood Press, 1997.

KARSON, JILL, ed. *Readings on* THE PEARL. San Diego: Greenhaven Press, 1999.

MEYER, MICHAEL J., ed. *The Betrayal of Brotherhood in the Work of John Steinbeck.* Lewiston, New York: Edwin Mellen Press, 2000.

STEINBECK, JOHN. *Steinbeck: A Life in Letters* (new edition). New York: Penguin, 2001.

SWISHER, CLARICE, ed. *Readings on John Steinbeck.* San Diego: Greenhaven Press, 1996.